Praise for

The Serious Pursuit of Happiness
by Henry S. Miller

"Happiness is not something that happens. You have to actively pursue it. Sure, that bluebird may fly through your open window every now and then, but it's not likely to bless you very often unless you're proactive in achieving it. If you want to thrive, you have to strive. That's why Henry Miller's *The Serious Pursuit of Happiness* is a 'must-read.' Based on his extensive review of happiness research — no easy task in itself — Miller has identified six imperatives to thriving and flourishing at home and at work, and he offers up credible, sensible, and practical advice on how to apply what he's discovered. It's a bright gem of a book that shines light on the most significant actions you need to take every day to add more joy and well-being to your life."

JIM KOUZES

Award-winning coauthor of *The Leadership Challenge*, and Dean's Executive Fellow of Leadership, Leavey School of Business, Santa Clara University

"Here is a book packed with timeless advice. Organized for easy consumption and reference, *The Serious Pursuit of Happiness* is full of digestible kernels of wisdom."

PATRICK LENCIONI

President, The Table Group and author of *The Five Dysfunctions of a Team*

"Part recipe book, part tour guide, part bible, *The Serious Pursuit of Happiness* is a valuable companion to a successful life. Miller has made it extremely easy for those of us who are serious about happiness to find practical solutions that can help us achieve our goal. A 'must-read' if you are serious about flourishing, a complete waste of time if you're not."

LEWIS SCHIFF

Author, *The Middle-Class Millionaire*

"Amazing power in such an easy to read book. Miller has taken the psychology research on happiness and well-being and synthesized it down into its essential roadmap. All we have to do is 'just do it.'"

JOHN J. BOWEN JR.

Founder and CEO, CEG Worldwide, LLC and coauthor, *Breaking Through: Building a World-Class Wealth Management Business*

"Regardless of how happy you are, this book can help you increase your happiness quotient. Densely packed with practical ideas - it is a true synthesis of the best science and philosophy have to offer. I found myself pausing often to underline ideas, and in many cases I put the book down to go do something it recommended. How often can you say that about something you read? This is not a book to just be read, but a guide you will want to refer to on a regular basis."

RON CROSSLAND

Author, *Voice Lessons* and coauthor, *The Leaders Voice*

"Happiness, like any other worthwhile pursuit, takes time, understanding and commitment. Henry Miller has now given all who read this book the tools and a roadmap to a happier life. No more excuses; it's all here."

PATRICIA J. ABRAM

Financial Services Executive and coauthor, *Breaking Through: Building a World-Class Wealth Management Business*

"Everyone who wants to be happy (that would be you) should read this inspiring book; and then—since Henry Miller is one of the happiest and most indomitable people I've ever met—I'd highly recommend you do exactly as he says."

STEVE FARBER

Author, *The Radical Leap Re-Energized* and *Greater Than Yourself* President, Extreme Leadership, Inc.

THE **SERIOUS** PURSUIT OF

Happiness

*Everything You Need to Know
to Flourish and Thrive*

Henry S. Miller

WISDOM HOUSE MEDIA
LOS GATOS, CALIFORNIA

No part of this publication may be reproduced, stored in or introduced into a retrieval system, or transmitted, in any form or by any means (electronic, mechanical, photocopying, recording, or otherwise), without the prior written permission of the publisher. Contact: Wisdom House Media, P.O. Box 1537, Los Gatos, California 95031.

This publication is designed to provide accurate and authoritative information in regard to the subject matter covered. The advice and strategies contained herein may not be suitable for every situation. This book is sold with the understanding that neither the publisher nor the author are engaged in rendering professional services. If professional advice or other expert assistance is required, the services of a competent professional should be sought. Neither the publisher nor the author shall be held liable for damages arising from the misuse of any of the content.

Library of Congress Control Number: 2011929845

Miller, Henry S.
    The Serious Pursuit of Happiness: Everything You Need to Know to Flourish and Thrive / Henry S. Miller.
        xiv, 208 p., lc20.32 cm.
        ISBN 978-1-937071-00-4

1. Happiness, 2. Conduct of life,
3. Positive psychology, 4. Self-actualization (psychology),
5. Success, 6. Leadership
I. Title. II. Miller, Henry S.

First Paperback Edition

Book and cover design by Mark Gelotte, www.markgelotte.com

This book is dedicated to the joys of my life:
Evelyn, Nicole, Emma, Abby, Kirk, Rick,
"Rip," and the Mig.

CONTENTS

PHASE III
PLAN AND ACT

Ⓗ

THE **SERIOUS** PURSUIT OF

Happiness

*Everything You Need to Know
to Flourish and Thrive*

PREFACE

Most people, when asked if they would like to be happier, reply along these lines:

"Sure. Just tell me what to do!"

And that's exactly what this book does. I have deliberately written it to be a prescriptive, one-stop happiness shop with everything you need to know to begin living a happier and more fulfilling life—all simply organized into six imperatives and all presented in one small, companion-sized book.

My goal in writing is also simple: to help people live happier lives—to flourish—beginning now. As you read, absorb the knowledge and recommended actions packed into virtually every page. And, after you finish reading, be confident that, no matter what manner of circumstance exists now or may befall you as you navigate the future chapters of your life, you will possess all the proven strategies, key insights, and tested actions necessary to live a fuller and more meaningful life.

The ultimate promise of the book is to provide you—all simply set forth in one place—with *everything* psychologists, researchers, and other scientists around the world have found that people need to know to thrive. This promise assures that the paths and actions recommended here are all substantively research-based and can be counted upon to reliably deliver the desired result—a happier life.

The underlying premise of the book is just as important: if presented with the specific actions for a happier life and if—and this is the big *if*—willing to implement these actions in their day-to-day lives, almost everyone can increase their level of happiness starting today—and often in a lasting way.

The approach has been to "research the research" and then use the findings as the basis for the writing. Think of this research as a three-legged stool:

- Published findings from over four decades of happiness research encompassing hundreds of studies of many thousands of people from all around the world.

- Latest advances and research study findings from the newest branch of psychology, *positive psychology,* which is the scientific study of what is good about people and life and how it can be made more fulfilling—as distinguished from traditional psychology's focus on what is wrong with people and how to best heal them.

- Latest breakthroughs in biology, genetics, and neuroscience—specifically as they affect our ability to be happier.

My contribution has been to synthesize the results from these three legs of research together into this one book. And this synthesis has revealed an astounding consensus of thought on what psychologists and researchers from around the world have found—to live happier and more fulfilling lives, people need to follow six imperatives:

- The First Imperative: Seek Pleasure within Limits.
- The Second Imperative: Intentionally *Think* Happy.
- The Third Imperative: Intentionally *Act* Happy.
- The Fourth Imperative: Become a Better Person.
- The Fifth Imperative: Embrace Loving Connections.
- The Sixth Imperative: Make a Meaningful Contribution.

These imperatives are so powerful that you can turn to almost any page in Phase Two of the book and immediately feel inspired to change. The strategies that make up each imperative are clear and practical, making it easy to feel more motivated to transcend your reality and to seek to live a happier and more fulfilling life.

Reading the book will give you a clear road map to a happier future. But having the map is just the beginning. It's necessary to actually embark on the journey to a happier life. To facilitate this essential step, the book also includes chapters on how to construct your personal happiness plan and how to manage your limited time to implement your life-changing happiness opportunities long after your reading is done.

And, in case you would like to delve deeper to obtain a more detailed understanding of the research-based findings and studies on which this book is based, I have included in the Appendix a suggested readings list and a starter list of significant studies—all of which form the scientific foundation that supports the recommendations presented in the book.

Please enjoy your journey.

(H)

INTRODUCTION

> ✳ *By three methods we may learn wisdom: first, by reflection, which is noblest, second, by imitation, which is easiest, and third, by experience, which is the most bitter.*
>
> —Confucius, Chinese philosopher and teacher
> (557?–479 B.C.)

Once people in civilized nations around the globe reach a level of development where their basic needs are met— air, food and water, shelter, safety and security, a feeling of belonging, and enough money to rise above the poverty line— then their thoughts often turn to concerns of a higher order: the age-old questions of happiness, the meaning of life, and the realization of their potential. Since the beginning of time, individuals the world over have forged their destinies and fulfilled their dreams using a simple but powerful three-stage process: study and reflection followed by well-considered plans culminating in focused action. This straightforward, proven process can be applied with great effect to any significant and worthwhile endeavor.

For those who choose to embark on or continue their life-long journey in pursuit of a happier life, this book provides an easy-to-follow, three-phase road map. It is replete with detailed strategies and specific actions based on scientific research about how to be happier—all synthesized down into six imperatives to implement in your own life. Think of the pages to follow as a robust menu based on tested recipes for increasing your level of happiness. All you need to do is to select the entrées that seem most appetizing and add them to the banquet of experience that forms your day-to-day life.

Let this book be both your compass and your faithful companion on your journey to a happier life. This journey—like most journeys—has three distinct and logical phases:

- Phase One: Preparation to ensure your readiness,

- Phase Two: Proven Paths to present the six imperatives to follow for a happier life, and

- Phase Three: Plan and Act to create and then implement your personal happiness plan.

Begin—or continue—your pursuit of happiness, confident that you have in your possession everything you need to live a happier life. Remember that, for all of us, when the wild rollicking rumpus of life winds down, we *are* the choices we've made each day along the way.

Be bold. Begin your journey now.

$$\textcircled{H}$$

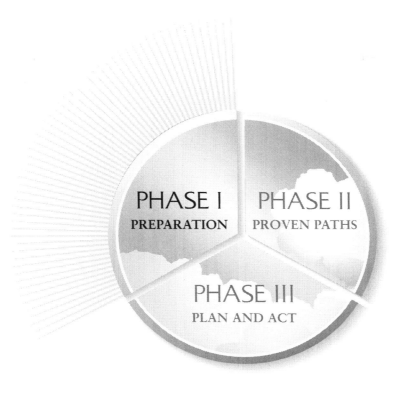

PHASE I
PREPARATION

PHASE II
PROVEN PATHS

PHASE III
PLAN AND ACT

PREPARATION

✗ To be prepared is half the victory.

— Miguel de Cervantes Saavedra, Spain's greatest literary
figure, author of *Don Quixote* (1547–1616)

Proper preparation presages success. This first phase of our journey to create a sustainably happier and more fulfilling life includes a call to action, a brief synopsis of the history of this epic pursuit, a definition of what happiness is—and what it is not, some views on why happiness matters, and the three major determinants that circumscribe the boundaries of our happiness potential. Completing the preparation process is an introduction to the major keys for a successful journey—the keys to the kingdom. These keys include both the capabilities inherent in each human being and a reminder that nothing great in life is ever achieved without desire, dedication, and effort.

CHAPTER 1

A RACE TO BE RUN

Nothing can bring you happiness but yourself.

— Ralph Waldo Emerson, American essayist,
philosopher, and poet (1803–1882)

Commit to seeking a happier life for yourself. The pursuit of happiness, it turns out, is a challenge—a contest, a race that all of us can actually win—rather than a mere whim of fate that we can only hope for. The six imperatives introduced in the Preface and discussed in detail in Phase Two brightly light the paths that lead to a happier life.

Historically, there has been a time-honored view about happiness—that "the bluebird of happiness" may fly in the window if we leave it open. Similarly, Nathaniel Hawthorne memorably said: "Happiness is a butterfly, which, when pursued, is always just beyond your grasp, but which, if you sit down quietly, may alight upon you." These passive views about happiness, eloquent as they are, have turned out to be false.

The relatively new science of positive psychology—one of the three legs of happiness research analyzed for you here—is proving that each of us can and should take positive steps on a journey to actively implement the six imperatives. And we don't have to wait until the end of our journey to feel happier. An added incentive is that each step, no matter how small, brings with it an immediate boost in feelings of well-being. This motivates us to take the next step on the journey. And the next. And the one after that.

THREE CAVEATS

As you begin your journey, three caveats merit thoughtful consideration:

First, some of the proven recommended actions in the six imperatives for living a happier life will be so familiar—so similar to the time-honored advice you received from your parents and grandparents—that you might think, "Of course, I knew that." Please remember, just because you've heard some of these platitudes for most of your life, don't let that historical familiarity—what is termed "hindsight bias"—cause you to discount or dismiss their power. These ways of thinking, acting, being, and doing can absolutely increase the amount of happiness in your life. In hindsight, most universal truths seem like common sense—something that we each knew to be true. Instead of being sidetracked by "I knew it all along" smugness, be confident that a happier life is closer and more achievable than ever because of this foreknowledge.

Second, some of the recommended actions in the six imperatives may surprise you. If so, don't be dismayed or dismissive. Stay open-minded about the proven paths that are offered— they have helped millions of people live happier lives, and they can help you do the same.

Whatever your reaction, be assured that all six imperatives are implementable in some form by everyone. For maximum success on your journey, focus your limited time and energy on those imperatives and their strategies and proven actions that yield the longest-lasting feelings of happiness and forego other familiar paths, no matter how tempting. Your goal is to learn, understand, and internalize the recommendations in these six imperatives and then create and implement your own personal happiness plan for a better life.

Third, the research demonstrates conclusively that there is no one single factor—no one "secret"—that is both necessary and sufficient for a happier life. The pursuit of happiness is more complex than that. Instead of just one "secret" way, you have multiple paths that you can follow. In fact, implementing *any* of the recommended actions in *any* of the six imperatives has been proven to increase levels of happiness. The scientific study of well-being on which this book is based can help you rethink your priorities and how you allocate your time each hour of each day of each week for the rest of your life.

A KEY REMINDER

The most frequent factor that keeps people from living happier lives is a failure to change their thinking and their attitudes and ultimately their actions. They fail in the most essential task of all: to incorporate the proven thinking and recommended actions that lead to a happier life into the way they live each and every day on an ongoing basis. There are many reasons for this failure—often it is due in part to the levels of anxiety and depression rampant in our societies today. No matter what the reasons, however, trust that—except in extreme cases—the human condition can be improved by intelligently applying the advice in this book. Each and every statement is based on solid findings about actions to take that will not only make you happier but also healthier, more productive, better married, and longer lived.

IN THE END

Life can be viewed as a roller-coaster ride down a long and winding path that is sometimes only dimly lighted to an often unclear destination. And, for those who do not believe in an afterlife, this destination is ultimately a dead end. We each eventually must come to terms with the paradox that life seems at once critically urgent and yet ultimately pointless. And, even though many of life's chapters begin as mysteries without many clues, the life we are living today is not just a trial run. We need to make the most of our time on the planet while we can.

Don't die wondering why your life turned out the way it did—and whether or not it could have been better. A happier life awaits those who choose to pursue implementation of the six happiness imperatives outlined in these pages. There is confidence and freedom and power in the realization that many of the solutions and proven paths to a happier life seem almost timeless. Just investing a small amount of reading time now can jump-start a lifelong journey to win the ultimate prize: a flourishing, thriving, happier, and more meaningful life.

CHAPTER 2

WHAT HAPPINESS IS

Happiness is the meaning and purpose of life, the whole aim and end of human existence.

—Aristotle, Greek philosopher, pupil of Plato
(384–322 B.C.)

A brief look around reveals that happiness is often portrayed as a simple, sometimes even trivialized topic. Smiley faces, "Happy" perfume from Clinique, the Bobby McFerrin song "Don't Worry, Be Happy," the movie *The Pursuit of Happyness,* and the Coca-Cola advertisement to "open happiness" are but a few examples of the commercialization of the concept.

Yet, in spite of frequent and popular oversimplification, happiness remains one of the most highly prized yet most frequently misunderstood states of mind—hard to define, hard to find, and harder to sustain. Almost everyone in the civilized world has spent some portion of life searching for happiness. In fact, if you ask the average person what he or she wants most out of life, the most likely reply will be: "I just want to be happy." Indeed, over the centuries, it is both the most sought-after condition of human existence and the most tantalizingly elusive. From Aristotle to Cicero to Buddha to Confucius to the Dalai Lama to the United Nations to the U.S. Declaration of Independence to modern-day positive psychology—people have constantly pondered and wondered and written about happiness. Sometimes we wonder if it is a goal we are destined never to reach no matter how hard we try—like perpetual motion or eternal youth.

THE DEFINITION OF WHAT HAPPINESS IS

Many opinions about what happiness is have been voiced throughout history. Yet, so far, there is no one magic wand to instantly create lasting happiness nor is there a simple "happiness thermometer" to help measure it. The good news is that science has now taken a role to help both by defining this elusive state of being and by recommending the best routes to follow to achieve and then sustain it in lasting and even lifelong ways.

First, social scientists now mostly agree on a definition: happiness is *subjective well-being*. Simply put, each of us is exactly as happy as we think we are and say we are when asked. And these same scientists have now measured people's level of happiness reliably by using what is termed "self-reported subjective well-being"—which means letting people record how happy they're feeling by answering a simple questionnaire. This definition has been validated as being accurate.

Second, there is corroboration from the field of biology. Happiness isn't just some vague, ineffable feeling, it is an observable physical state of the brain—one that can be induced deliberately. Measurable biological results solidly confirm the validity of "self-reported subjective well-being." Since emotions are in fact biological events, happy people display specific patterns of brain activity. According to a field called *affective neuroscience,* positron emission tomography (PET) scans have demonstrated that the left prefrontal cortex of the human brain—the area associated with positive emotions—lights up when people are feeling happy. This area is often cited as the prime locus of happiness.

The Long and the Short of It

If you reflect for a moment about what makes you happy, your "self-reported subjective well-being" includes two different durations of feelings: the bursts of pleasurable experiences resulting in positive emotions that make you feel happy for a short time and the deeper feelings of well-being, contentment, and satisfaction with life in general. These more underlying feelings that life is good, purposeful, worthwhile, and satisfying—that life has meaning—are more sustainable and longer-lasting than the mere simple bursts of pleasure.

Almost everyone, hopefully, has experienced both these types of happiness at some point in life. And that experience is borne out by the research: short-term pleasure certainly makes people feel happy, even euphoric. But sustainable happiness requires depth and people and meaning in a life. Neither pleasure bursts nor the deeper feelings alone are sufficient, but both together can be rewarding and reinforcing by evoking feelings of happiness in different ways and for varying lengths of time. When we work hard and even struggle while working toward a worthy goal—one that has intrinsic meaning for us—our happiness is increased. Certainly enjoying pleasure while in an activity can make it all the more meaningful, but it is often the struggle that makes the end result all the more worthwhile. Happiness, therefore, has both a present, short-term feeling and benefit and a longer-term, more lasting feeling of meaningful enjoyment. Our life experiences of feeling both intense joy and a deeper feeling of underlying contentment with ourselves and our life validate this scientific definition.

THE THREE MAJOR DETERMINANTS OF HAPPINESS

If "self-reported subjective well-being" is the definition of happiness, and if these feelings are generated by both short-lasting pleasurable feelings of joy and longer-lasting, deeper feelings of satisfaction, contentment, and meaning—and if both of these feelings have been validated by studies of brain chemistry, then what determines how we experience these feelings? Leading psychologists the world over now believe people's level of happiness—their "self-reported subjective well-being"—is determined by three major factors:

- Genetic Inheritance
- Environment and Life Circumstances
- Happiness-Increasing Thoughts and Actions

Genetic Inheritance

Heredity happens to each of us, like it or not. And, although it may initially come as a surprise to you (it certainly surprised me), part of the capacity for happiness is in our genes.

Some of us are just born happier than others.

Each of us is born with our own unique genetic predis-position for a certain level of sustainable happiness that we can't change beyond certain limits—call it an internal "hap-piness thermostat" setting, if you wish. A growing number of relatively recent studies of identical and fraternal twins have unequivocally established that we each have a "set point" or a "set range" of happiness that we are given at birth, the most notable of which is David Lykken's and Auke Tellegen's 1996 ground-breaking study at the University of Minnesota using data from the Minnesota Twin Registry. This is nature (as in the old nature-versus-nurture debate) playing a role. In the same way that we inherit a familiar and proven predisposition for height and weight from our biological parents, psychologists have estimated that this genetic happiness inheritance accounts for about *half* of our overall normal level of happiness. Interestingly, this moderate 50 percent level of happiness heritability is similar to the moderate heritability levels of personality, intelligence, and susceptibility to Alzheimer's disease—far higher than the mere three percent heritability for life span but far lower than more highly heritable traits such as height, body weight, ADHD, and bipolar disorder (which approach 70–90+ percent). As with optimism, loneliness, extroversion, depression, and other inherited characteristics, everyone receives some predisposition to be a certain level of happy.

Once our thinking moves beyond the newness and maybe even the shock of this new genetic reality, our "happiness thermostat"—preset at birth—turns out to be both good and bad news for each of us.

The Good News

The good news is there is now some rational explanation for the way some people always seem down or sad compared to those who always seem so happy and upbeat. Discovering that we each have an inherent level of happiness that is genetically predetermined provides some relief and comfort by neatly explaining this common observation: some people are naturally happier or unhappier than others. This makes sense and, for some—particularly those of us who have struggled through various efforts to be happier in our lives—it's a relief to know there's maybe nothing wrong with us: that's just the way we are.

Another part of the good news about this genetically set "happiness thermostat" is that, in the face of hardship and loss and their constant companions, pain and suffering, we can still feel comforted and confident that, after experiencing all but the most extreme lows of life, no matter how unhappy we may feel in the moment, over time we can expect with some certainty to return naturally to our normal baseline inherited level of well-being—our "set point" or "set range" of happiness. It can be reassuring when science confirms what we've observed and often experienced to be the case. And, in this case, we are often relieved in a way to find out that our dogged resilience in the face of the human trials and tribulations that come to all of us has some basis in scientific findings.

And there's more good news: even if we seem to be on the low end of the genetic happiness scale, our genetic starting point should not be cause for feelings of futility. Even though science now suggests a fixed "set range" for a level of happiness that is circumscribed by our genetic inheritance, it turns out that personality traits are *not* as strongly hardwired as other traits like eye color, height, and weight, so that feelings like happiness *can* be lastingly increased. Heritability does not mean immutability.

The six imperatives of Phase Two are devoted to demonstrating that with focused effort, we each can rise above our genetic inheritance to live a happier life in the upper level of our "set range."

The Bad News

The bad news, of course, is that this genetic "happiness thermostat" means that the ability to increase the level of happiness is not as unlimited as we may have hoped—or as previous decades of positive thinking without scientific foundation have had many of us believing. Instead, it is more limited—even though certainly not nonexistent—because there are now genetic boundaries to what has been termed *human plasticity*—or what was thought to be human beings' almost unlimited ability to change almost everything about themselves if they just worked at it hard enough. Still, all is not lost. We are quite able to increase our levels of happiness sufficiently to live sustainably happier lives, once we know what to do.

Environment and Life Circumstances

As you might suspect from the familiar nature-and-nurture discussions, nurture also imposes limitations on the human potential for happiness. Past experiences, current life circumstances, and demographics—age, race, gender, education, where we live—all also influence each person's preset range of happiness, but not nearly as much as you might imagine. This second limitation—which psychologists estimate accounts for only maybe *a tenth* (10 percent) of the predisposition for happiness—includes your life circumstances: your past and present environment, including where you grew up, the major positive and negative events of your childhood and life right up to the present, your current resources (income or assets and material possessions), your age, gender, ethnicity, appearance, marital status, education, and specific occupation, your religious affiliation if you have one, your neighborhood, your living conditions, your health (including whether or not you have a chronic or acute illness). All that: 10 percent only.

Happiness-Increasing Thoughts and Actions

The final factor influencing the level of happiness you experience in your life is up to you to determine. No matter how long or short your genetic leash may be and no matter what challenges your upbringing left you to deal with or how stressful or pleasant your current situation may be, it has been conclusively demonstrated that, within some limitations, you can increase your happiness potential. By choosing to be more deliberately intentional about who you are as a person and by guiding your own thoughts and actions—that is, by consciously directing your life in proven positive directions—you can affect *slightly less than half*—estimates say 40 percent—of your potential level of well-being, often in sustainable, long-lasting ways. By observing happy people and learning their habits, you can use their attitudes, behavior, and life situations as a guide for your own intentional thoughts and actions.

The six imperatives that are the core of this book are focused on these sustainable happiness-increasing strategies—pursuing both pleasure and more meaningful activities that can significantly raise your level of well-being in the short term (minutes and hours), the medium term (days, weeks, and months), and for the long term (years and for life).

VALIDATION

On a macro level, to validate both the definition of happiness and the influence of these three major happiness determinants, dozens of researchers around the world have surveyed more than a million people—a representative sample of the human race. Interestingly, the results from people's self-reported subjective well-being remain, in psychologist-speak, "moderately consistent over the years." The stability in these findings indicates the influence of enduring traits like genetic inheritance and life circumstances—both upbringing and current situation. Meanwhile, the variation in the findings indicates the influence of recent life events such as any positive thinking and positive actions that people choose to deliberately incorporate into their day-to-day life to increase the feelings of happiness.

OPPORTUNITY

While slightly more than half—60 percent—of your level of happiness may be predestined, the remaining *40 percent* is up to you to determine. Once you've accepted and adjusted to this new reality, however, it is your responsibility to dedicate yourself to moving beyond and above your preset level of well-being potential. Unless you choose to determinedly cling to the pain of your past or present, you have ample—though not unlimited—opportunity to choose to live in the upper region of your "set range" of happiness by adopting certain proven ways of thinking, acting, and being.

As difficult as it may be to imagine and accept, no matter what your nature-and-nurture legacy, your chances of living a happier life are still, in large part, up to you to determine.

CHAPTER 3

WHY HAPPINESS MATTERS

There is no duty we so much underrate as the duty of being happy.

—Robert Louis Stevenson, Scottish novelist, poet, and essayist (1850–1894)

Although some would have you think otherwise, the uniquely human pursuit of happiness is not merely some frivolous idle-time activity for the fortunate few. Far from it. Instead, it is a serious pursuit—a duty and responsibility for each of us.

As the progress—or lack thereof—of human evolution has demonstrated, being in a positive, optimistic, and happy frame of mind seems to be what allows some humans to be more successful than others in obtaining life's essentials: food, shelter, social support, even a mate. So it has always been and so it continues today. And if you still doubt the seriousness of pursuing a happier life, consider your loved ones. Fulfilling the duty of being happy benefits not just yourself but also those closest to you.

The Benefits

Most of the benefits of living a happier life are familiar, yet they are powerful and seemingly endless—and they far outweigh the costs and work needed to achieve this state. Nonetheless, many in our societies often try to diminish the idea of simple, lasting happiness, instead extolling the thrill of peak pleasures and magnificent accomplishments. As a rejoinder to them and a reminder to us all, here is a consensus of what researchers around the world (including those cited in the Suggested Readings list in the Appendix) have proven to result from simply being happy, especially when compared to unhappy, sad, or depressed people:

- *Success.* Overall, happy people are more successful across multiple major domains of life including work, social relationships, income, and health. In addition, the relationship between happiness and success seems to be reciprocal: not only can individual success—whether in love or at work—contribute to feelings of happiness, but happiness also results in more success. In this way, happiness becomes an even more worthwhile pursuit, both as a desirable end in and of itself and as a means to achieve other significant life goals.

- *Personally.* Happy people more frequently exhibit characteristics such as being strikingly energetic, decisive, and flexible. They are more creative, more helpful to those in need, more self-confident, more forgiving, more charitable, more sociable, and more loving. Compared to unhappy people, happier people are more trusting, more loving, and more responsive. They have greater self-control, can tolerate frustration better, are less likely to be abusive, are more lenient, and demonstrate enhanced coping skills.

- *Socially.* Happy people have more friends, richer social interactions, correspondingly stronger social support, and experience longer and more satisfying marriages.

- *Work.* In addition to bringing all their positive personal attributes to work, happy people have been proven to be more likely to perform better, achieve greater productivity and deliver a higher quality work product. They tend to receive a higher income as a result.

- *Physical health.* Happy people experience less pain, are often in better health, are more active with more energy, and even, not surprisingly, live longer. They have lower stress levels and stronger immune systems that fight disease more effectively. By comparison, stressed and depressed people are more vulnerable to various illnesses.

- *Mental health.* Happy individuals construe daily situations and major life events in relatively more positive and more adaptive ways that seem to reinforce their happiness. They are also less likely to exaggerate any criticism, however slight, that they may receive, as opposed to unhappy individuals who react to life experiences in negative ways that only reinforce their unhappiness.

NOT A ONE-NIGHT READ

With these benefits in mind, it is clear this book is not intended to be just a one-night read. Taking this initial step of reading the book, while essential, is not enough. Instead, reading and learning and being inspired are merely the first steps of a lifelong journey. Choosing to actually implement the six imperatives into your life—and to take advantage of the following keys—is your ticket to the happier life you desire.

CHAPTER 4

THE KEYS TO THE KINGDOM

No one can cheat you out of ultimate success but yourself.
—Ralph Waldo Emerson, American essayist,
philosopher, and poet (1803–1882)

After every experience—whether a triumph or disaster—we look back and say, mostly to ourselves: "If only I knew then what I know now, I would have done things differently." The journey to live a happier life is no different—except that, as a result of this chapter, you will have the advantage of foreknowledge instead of the regret of hindsight.

These are the seven keys to the kingdom:
- Self-Reliance and Related Keys.
- No Pain, No Gain.
- The Forces Are With You—Like It or Not.
- New Habits.
- Self-Focused to Other-Focused.
- House Brand.
- Destiny.

Take them all to heart—they will be decisive in unleashing the potential of the six imperatives. By focusing on their importance and internalizing them now—before beginning your quest for happiness, you will gain a huge head start to enhance your chances for a successful journey.

SELF-RELIANCE AND RELATED KEYS

Rely on yourself to create your own happier life. "If it's going to be, it's up to me" is more than just a catchy saying. Self-reliance—relying on your own capabilities, judgment, and resources—is essential to taking deliberate action to successfully deploy the six happiness imperatives.

Harness the power of your will to make a happier life a priority. Rely on the power of perseverance to live your life differently in spite of distractions and the intrusions of old familiar habits. Value yourself and your happiness. So much of what happens in life is about will—that internal agent that triggers your mind and body to engage in purposeful activity. Have you noticed? Will is key to all successful, significant human endeavors and undertakings—school, marriage, relationships, careers—and is the critical factor in helping guide people to do the right thing according to their conscience and to avoid being distracted from following the proven paths to a happier life.

Of course, for many of us, self-reliance, personal responsibility, and relying on willpower to accomplish goals are familiar concepts—this is just how we are. But for others, the thought of self-reliance is fraught with doubt and fear. The antidotes are straightforward. First, share your goal of living a happier life with close confidants—just confiding in someone else can diminish doubt, stress, and fear. Ask for the support of people who have your best interests at heart. Second, have faith in the recommended actions—and just go ahead and do them until they become habits. At least, try them once or twice. And, third, remind yourself that the long-term benefits of a happier life far outweigh the immediate anxiety you may feel by having to try unfamiliar thinking and new actions.

Remember, not only can you live more happily for the rest of your life, you can feel immediately happier as you begin your journey. The moment you choose to rely on yourself and exercise your will to work toward a happier life—to act as the agent of change—you will feel elevated and inspired and filled with joy and pride. This boost of positive feeling is vital—it buoys your spirits throughout the journey—and it can be continually renewed after every action you take to make these imperatives a part of your life from now on. Taking personal responsibility for your happiness and employing your strength of will to engage in happiness-increasing activities is also the antidote to dooming yourself to being a *victim*—and lets you avoid the pain that role inevitably brings.

So, rely on you. Choose to take personal responsibility for your happiness-producing choices and to commit yourself—to *will* yourself—to take action. These are key prerequisites for increasing your happiness. They are also the hallmarks of fully integrated, fully functioning adult human beings.

NO PAIN, NO GAIN

Embrace the truth of the adage "no pain, no gain." Every significant, worthwhile human endeavor—whether it involves school, relationships, or career—takes significant effort and sometimes, at least initially, some plain old hard work to reap a correspondingly significant and often lifelong reward.

The pursuit of a lastingly happier and more fulfilling life is no different.

There is no happiness pill, no one magic secret that will effortlessly bring anyone lasting happiness. Wishing to be happier is not enough. As with exercise, weight loss, or smoking cessation programs, dedication, focus, and sustained work are needed for success. Don't wait for the mythical bluebird of happiness to alight on your shoulder. Work to create your own happier life—beginning now. The choice is yours: long-lasting happiness is effortful, not effortless.

THE FORCES ARE WITH YOU—LIKE IT OR NOT

Be cognizant of and alert for two major psychological forces: adaptation and social comparison. Both are ubiquitous and difficult to avoid. And, separately and together, they have a major impact on the potential success of any journey to live a happier life. Cultivate the ability to recognize when they are in play and, most important, adjust your happiness-increasing plans accordingly.

Adaptation

The first psychological force affecting happiness is *adaptation* —the remarkable human ability to adjust to changes in life circumstances. People generally can become accustomed to almost any new situation—often quite rapidly. Whether the change is a triumph or a tragedy—a lottery win, a Nobel Prize, or a lost job, a divorce, or even paralysis from a car accident—people always seem, over varying lengths of time, to be able to adjust—to return to their previous (and partly genetically determined) "set range" of happiness. Every event or experience—whether a high or a low—is temporary. They all fade—and then we bounce back up from a valley and fall back down after a peak. Both extremes—elation and dejection—are impossible to sustain for long.

The significance of this adaptation process cannot be overemphasized. Most important, adaptation works in both directions. No matter what happens to your objective life circumstances—for better or worse—once you've adapted to it, your new situation bears little relation to your happiness—it's just your "new normal."

The Good News

The good news about adaptation is you can adapt even when bad things happen in your life. Awareness of this innate ability to adapt is reassuring: allowing you to be confident that, in time, you will recover your former level of happiness—as if you had some form of internal happiness thermostat—which you do. For all except the most extreme life situations and events (such as death of a child, rape, child abuse, combat, and concentration camp internment), adaptation works to help restore former levels of happiness. As my mother was fond of saying, "You can get used to almost anything except a tack in your shoe."

The Bad News

The bad news—from a happiness standpoint—is that you will also adapt to the good things that happen to you. This means that many popular, glorified paths to happiness—the constant seeking of more and more fun and pleasurable experiences, the avoidance of pain, and the accumulation of more money and more material things, among others—are all doomed to fail as long-term happiness-producing strategies. People adapt. No matter how much pleasure or fun or money or "stuff" we amass, we adapt. And, often surprisingly soon, these cease to produce their original feelings of joy.

Social Comparison

The second psychological force affecting happiness is called *social comparison*. You will probably find this force familiar, whether or not you have heard the term: it's our normal human tendency to compare ourselves with others. We compare in two directions—to those above us (upward comparison) on any scale imaginable (money, material possessions such as house or car, appearance, career success, intelligence, toys, and so on) and to those below us (downward comparison). We all are guilty of social comparison. We almost can't help it. Advertisers use it to their advantage to bombard us with claims such as: "If you want to look (or be) like this, use our product! Just buy it and see!" More specific to your happiness journey, though, is this reality: depending on your choice of comparison direction, you can deliberately cause yourself to feel better or worse. Enter the good, the bad, and the ugly:

The Good

Sometimes upward comparisons can be an inspiration to improve weaknesses and to strive for more ambitious goals. Rising aspirations occur often in response to upward comparisons, and are essential. In fact, without upward comparisons, we might tend to be content to dwell at our initial plateau of success to which we have comfortably adapted—without motivation or drive to accomplish more. But seeing a virtuoso perform or a true expert plying a trade can motivate the rest of us mere mortals to work harder and strive for that level of excellence. These aspirations fuel our ambitions, our expectations, and ultimately our achievements.

The Bad

However, one danger in constant upward comparison is obvious: if other people have more, whatever we have will not be enough. This realization, if left unchecked, can cause us unending feelings of envy, frustration, anxiety, inferiority, failure, and loss of self-esteem. Even if we have a lot of things, inevitably there is always someone with more of whatever we are comparing. Sadly, doing well is not enough. We also want to do better than our peers. As you may have noticed, feelings of *status anxiety* run deep. From the standpoint of a happiness journey, envy and its related feelings are the enemy—no one can be envious and feel happy at the same time. Thus, constantly only comparing upward dooms us to unhappiness.

But there is also danger in constantly only comparing downward. Usually we compare downward when we feel down, threatened, demoralized—and comparing ourselves to those with less makes us feel better and uplifted. But downward comparisons can cut both ways: we may feel more fortunate and grateful for what we *do* have but we also may feel guilt for having more than others. So in addition to coping with feeling the envy and resentment from those who are less fortunate, we may also fear suffering the same fate, particularly in trying times.

The Ugly

Some people believe they must make others feel bad in order for them to feel better—causing them to actually relish others' downfall. Those who have just failed or been made to feel insecure sometimes tend to try to get even by disparaging the other person or the other group or, in sports, the other team. Disparaging a rival person or group can help alleviate self-doubt. Perversely, it helps to have others to look down on. But sadly, this truism also helps explain the dogged persistence of prejudice, bigotry, and discrimination in human society.

What to Do

Adaptation and social comparison have important ramifications for your happiness journey. These two forces have the potential to thwart your drive for a happier life unless you take direct action to fight against their effects. Particularly when working to improve the sustainable, proven paths to a happier life—character, relationships, or careers—it's necessary to intentionally and actively manage social comparisons. Choose your social comparisons intentionally—your feelings depend on to whom and to what you compare yourself. Balance your comparisons—consciously compare *both* upward and downward—so you have some balance in your assessments of your station in life.

Tell yourself to stop only comparing upward. Also include downward comparisons that breed gratitude for what you have or who you are—reminders of your relative good fortune—instead of envy for what you lack. Remember that no one has everything. Don't always just recall and compare to your peak experiences—remembered ecstasies may make everyday moments seem mundane. Also recall significant low moments in your life. Without occasional reminders of how bad things have been or could be again, it may be harder to fully appreciate what you have. Even better: set your own internal standards by which to judge yourself instead of just relentlessly comparing to others. Finally, take direct action to tackle whatever disparities you notice based on your social comparisons. Just initiating small improvements can improve happiness and self-regard.

NEW HABITS

Form new happiness-increasing habits. These five words are easy to say, but forming new habits is challenging to do. Many well-intentioned efforts at adding new happiness-increasing activities into daily life fail, not because of lack of commitment or effort or determination, but because the new thoughts and behaviors never turn into habits.

As you know, habits are formed by practice and repetition. In fact, *habitual* means you no longer have to make a decision to do certain actions. They no longer require conscious thought—they are just what you do.

Successfully forming new habits is a process:

1. Increase readiness to change by contemplating the benefits of changing.

2. Ponder the difficulties of the changes.

3. Set goals.

4. Take action to begin to change using appropriate rewards and punishments as reinforcement.

5. Maintain the change by continually taking steps to prevent a relapse.

Setting specific goals will add to your motivation, as will keeping a journal to record your progress. And, when assessing your progress, don't just focus on what you still need to do—take a moment to relish what you've already accomplished. To keep the change permanent, plan the changes necessary to incorporate your new habits into your ongoing lifestyle.

Most agree that new habits take between 17 and 21 days to form. After that time, not performing the new behaviors creates a sort of void; you feel uncomfortable, as if something is missing from your life, and that is often incentive enough to reinstate the new behaviors.

New habits are important. They offer hope for sustainable results from implementing the new happiness-increasing thinking and activities that are presented in the six imperatives. And everyone can form new habits. This truth liberates those of us with more modest genetic predilections for happiness from the fear that we cannot be happier no matter how hard we try. Although the naturally happier among us seem to have inherited many of these happy habits, forming new positive habits based on the six imperatives allows anyone to be confident that, with time and determination, they too can develop exactly the same thinking and behaviors—and the benefits will last just as long.

The challenge, then, as in other arenas of life, is to imitate success—in this case, to imitate innately happy people. To be happier, make the activities that happy people do naturally what *you* do habitually. By making the actions recommended in all six imperatives into new habits, you too can live a happier life, no matter how you've thought about this possibility up to now.

SELF-FOCUSED TO OTHER-FOCUSED

Move from being self-focused to being other-focused. One of life's great ironies is that people who dedicate large portions of their lives to selfishly making themselves happier are actually far less likely to be happy and fulfilled than are those who choose to devote their efforts to making *others* happy.

This book presents the six imperatives in the order of the durability of the feelings of happiness they engender—beginning with the short-term pleasures of the first imperative, continuing to the medium-term intentional thinking and acting of the second and third imperatives, and culminating in the longest-lasting feelings of becoming a better person in the fourth imperative, the unequalled feelings of connection in the fifth imperative, and the pursuit of meaningful contribution in the sixth and final imperative.

Accordingly, this increase in the length of time the feelings of happiness last corresponds to a subtle but critically important shift in the focus of thought, action, and time prioritization while implementing the six imperatives—*away from* what is sometimes a preoccupation with self, particularly in the first imperative, and *toward* more of a focus on other people in the remaining five imperatives.

Whether it is shifting time allocation away from self-centered pursuits to working actively to improve relationships with others (a spouse or friends or colleagues), to being a better person to others, to limiting idle time and using that time to pursue a meaningful calling that helps other people, the increased focus on others offers far greater potential for happiness than remaining myopically self-focused.

HOUSE BRAND

Create your own unique "house brand" of proven actions to live a happier life based on the six imperatives. This "house brand" of new thinking and new actions—by definition—will be uniquely your own. There is no one best route to becoming happier—people are all different. To optimize your chances for success, absorb the intellectual capital in this book, ponder your best course of action, and decide which specific set of meaningful new happiness-increasing strategies best suits your skills and talents. Capture these plans in your personal happiness plan and then implement them into your day-to-day life with newfound excitement, hope, and inspiration.

The choice of which route to take is yours and yours alone. By choosing to manage your own state of mind and discipline yourself to create and then implement your unique "house brand" of chosen actions, you can begin your personal journey to a happier life today, comfortable that your planned actions *fit* your situation and your happiness goals.

DESTINY

Whether or not people's personal potential is fulfilled often depends in large part simply on whether or not they are each willing to accept personal responsibility for and then bravely pursue their own destiny. It is this exercise of will and courage that can ultimately determine how happy a life we individually imagine and, by extension, what type of society we collectively create. Only you can choose whether to accept a lesser life or, instead, to decide which are the right paths to follow to realize *your* destiny—and reap the reward of a happier life in the process.

CHAPTER 5

WHAT HAPPINESS IS NOT

It's pretty hard to tell what does bring happiness; poverty and wealth have both failed.

—Frank McKinney "Kin" Hubbard,
American journalist (1868–1930)

For a successful journey to a happier life, it's not enough to just know what happiness *is*—you also need to be able to discern what it *is not*. Stop worshipping at the wrong altars. Let go of some of the false beliefs and myths about happiness that waste your precious time and distract you from investing your energy in implementing the six happiness imperatives.

THE DEFINITION OF WHAT HAPPINESS IS NOT

First, our potential for happiness is *not* unlimited. Instead, each individual's ability to live a happier life is constrained to varying degrees by uncontrollable factors—genetic propensities, upbringing, life circumstances. On the other hand, these limits on your ultimate happiness opportunity do not remotely block your ability to be happier than you are today.

Second, happiness is *not* about evading and escaping all pain and suffering for as long as possible so as to experience an unchanging plateau of positive emotion. That uninterrupted, dreamlike feeling of total bliss that will last forever—the constant high, the perpetual vacation that is the brass ring of happiness—is a fantasy. Expecting this type of happiness means denying the natural ups and downs and the peaks and valleys that are a part of every life. Living a full life means experiencing a full range of positive and negative emotions. Real life is full of minor inconveniences, major disappointments, and real loss. And, as a result, far from a continuous feeling of bliss—the level of human happiness from moment to moment is actually quite changeable—some say fleeting. Even the happiest among us have their share of problems and feel depressed at times—just as the depressed sometimes experience moments of joy and exhilaration that break through the clouds.

Instead of trying to limit your range of feelings to the upper end of the scale, it is better to confront your inevitable negative feelings head-on—without letting them overwhelm you. In reality, although it is often difficult to acknowledge in moments of loss, negative states can be important and useful: they provide cues to what is valuable and highlight what needs to change. Grief for loss of a loved one is a reminder to cherish other relationships. Frustration with a less-than-perfect job may be a clue that it's time to change careers. But, even in the inevitable valleys, it is still possible to feel that, overall, in spite of its normal ups and downs, life is basically happy. Often, without the contrast of sorrow and sadness, happiness would not be as sweet.

Third, common sense says that to have more happiness in

your life you should strive mightily to change, minimize, or avoid bad events that make you miserable. And, while being less miserable is certainly a good thing and worth the effort, just because you may have more than your share of misery doesn't mean you can't have a lot of happiness as well. The truth is that, even if you have a lot of negative emotion in your life, you are not remotely doomed to a joyless life—*if* you are willing to work at being happy. Similarly, but sadly, the reverse is also true: even if you have a lot of happiness in your life, you are only moderately protected from sorrow and sadness.

Fourth, your happiness is *not* conditional upon someone or something else. Examples include the classic "When he or she changes, then I can be happy" trap and the Shangri-La fantasy that "If only I had X, Y, and Z, then I could be happy." No one ever has it all. And, no matter what we *do* have, we will constantly adapt anyway. So don't wait for some future, magical, perfect moment (which can never be realized) to be happy. Your happiness is largely up to you to determine without conditions.

Fifth, to be happier, you do *not* need to analyze every detail of your past and understand its influence on you in the present. Although a popular approach and one that has value, it is also often a route to self-absorption and self-pity. We all have a past. Understanding that past is not an essential determinant of how happy you will be from now on, the six imperatives are.

Sixth, long-lasting happiness is *not* a matter of being a passive passenger partaking of the pleasures on the perpetual pleasure train. You will eventually adapt to all pleasures. Neither does it call for deferring all action in life while waiting for your specific God to intervene on your behalf. Instead, it requires acting as an agent of change on your life.

Finally, taking the laid-back lifestyle approach instead of the

Protestant work ethic won't work either. Deep inside, humans feel guilty about not striving—we know something is missing. And by choosing a constantly laid-back life, we also miss the many opportunities for happiness that come from working.

THE ROADS TO NOWHERE

Shun the blind pursuit of many of the most popularly accepted ideas of what makes people happy. The pursuit—even the successful pursuit—of more money, success, fame, power, beauty, talent, and material possessions has repeatedly been proven to be a failed road to lasting happiness.

One route to true wisdom is learning from the experiences of others. Heed the real "lessons from the rich and famous" to be derived from life in Hollywood and elsewhere. If the movie, music, and TV stars have anything to teach us, it is their real secret: limitless money, success, fame, power, and talent don't bring lasting happiness. Just observe the epidemic levels of depression and addiction, the ruined marriages and troubled children afflicting even the most successful of stars. Having external good things in abundance doesn't insulate anyone from their share—and sometimes more than their share—of misery. Ask yourself if Elvis, Marilyn, Janis, Kurt, River, Michael, Whitney, and a host of other celebrities died because their money, beauty, talent, success, and fame made them lastingly happy.

Just learning and accepting this one truth can be life-transforming—saving time and money while reducing the anguish of envy—courtesy of the stars. No matter how temptingly enjoyable a life devoted to these false idols may seem, remember: people always adapt. And the stars aren't the only people at risk of being seduced by these temptations. That new purchase, that big raise at work, that award or major promotion, that dream car or that dream house—at first are wonderful. You feel happy, even euphoric and ecstatic. But then, as time goes by, the newness fades, the excitement wanes, and what was new and wonderful becomes just the way life is. The new becomes the familiar and thus ceases to create the happiness it once did. No matter how fantastic something seems at first, it soon becomes just part of normal life.

In the face of this inevitable adaptation phenomenon, you have two options:

- Doggedly continue to strive to obtain more money, more possessions, more power, always more. There is no end to more. The problem is that, like children, when it comes to new toys, we have a short attention span. Or,

- Find another path. And the six imperatives are the routes to follow.

Speaking of money as a failed happiness-producer, according to the World Database of Happiness, although most of us on the planet are mostly happy, affluent countries from Japan to Australia to China to France to America haven't gotten much happier as they have grown wealthier. In the United States, as an example, we face the "paradox of plenty"—our wealth and income have increased dramatically over the past decades but our overall level of happiness as a nation has stayed virtually the same. At the same time, though, globally, people in wealthier nations—with some exceptions—*do* report themselves as feeling happier than people in poorer nations. It's clear—and only makes sense—that at least until life's necessities are comfortably taken care of, money plays some role in happiness. But, beyond having enough, the blind continued pursuit of money and success and possessions doesn't lead to significantly higher sustainable levels of happiness. In this way, wealth is like health: its utter absence breeds certain misery, but having it doesn't guarantee happiness. If we are truly honest with ourselves, our deepest yearnings are to make a difference to someone or something—to matter—not to just have more.

Pursuing more and more money, success, fame, and power is fine—admirable even—and an important goal of life if we choose: just don't expect lasting happiness as the guaranteed winner's prize. The innate tendency toward adaptation ensures that a focus on these things is guaranteed to fail as a long-term happiness-producing strategy. No matter how much you acquire, you will always *adapt* and take what you have for granted. This insight can be quite liberating. It allows you to open your eyes and focus your energies and time on implementing the six imperatives for flourishing while freeing you from staying tethered to a blind pursuit of these false roads to happiness—the roads to nowhere.

PHASE I
PREPARATION

PHASE II
PROVEN PATHS

PHASE III
PLAN AND ACT

PROVEN PATHS

A journey of a thousand miles begins with a single step.
— Lao Tzu, Chinese philosopher (600–531 B.C.)

Journeys tend to be more successful when the trail is clearly marked. This phase presents the proven paths—the six imperatives—that are the core strategies for a happier life in ascending order of durability—that is, how long-lasting are the feelings of happiness they create:

IMPERATIVE	DURATION
The First Imperative: **Seek Pleasure within Limits**	Short term (minutes, hours)
The Second Imperative: **Intentionally *Think* Happy**	Medium term (days, weeks, months)
The Third Imperative: **Intentionally *Act* Happy**	Medium term (days, weeks, months)
The Fourth Imperative: **Become a Better Person**	Long term (years, a lifetime)
The Fifth Imperative: **Embrace Loving Connections**	Long term (years, a lifetime)
The Sixth Imperative: **Make a Meaningful Contribution**	Long term (years, a lifetime)

Successfully implementing these six imperatives determines the remaining *slightly less than half*—40 percent—of your happiness that you control based on your choices. By focusing the majority of your limited time and energy on paths known to have the longest-lasting effect on your happiness—in some cases, a lifelong positive effect—you can boost your success at creating a lastingly happier life. It is no coincidence that, as the durability of happiness feelings increases, the imperatives are less focused on actions that satisfy the self and more focused on those that positively affect others. This shift is one of the "keys to the kingdom" and one of the true ironies about achieving lasting happiness: helping others often helps *you* more.

CHAPTER 6

THE FIRST IMPERATIVE:
SEEK PLEASURE WITHIN LIMITS

*The master of pleasure is not he who abstains from it
but he who uses it without being carried away by it.*

—Aristippus, Greek philosopher
(435?–356? B.C.)

By all means, seek out and partake of the pleasures in all their familiar forms—physical pleasures, fun, peak experiences, food and drugs—but do so within limits. Pleasure is an essential and quite enjoyable first imperative for living a happy life—even if primarily self-centered—yielding short-term bursts of happiness and often euphoria and even ecstasy. Allowing pleasurable feelings to wash over you like a waterfall of joy is the most obvious and perhaps the most reliably popular path to happiness of all. And even though these feelings don't last long—often only minutes or hours—it is only fitting that the six imperatives begin here.

THE PLEASURES

The pleasures of our lives can take an almost unlimited number of familiar forms. *Physical pleasures* are, of course, sensations: a delicious meal, a favorite dessert, a warm bath, your favorite chocolate, a fine cigar, a fantastic massage, a gratifying sexual experience. All can be blissful and all do tend to produce pleasure, suppress negative feelings, and induce calm, but only for a few moments—the happy feelings usually end when the pleasure ends.

Fun is similar. Fun activities certainly evoke feelings of happiness—going to amusement parks, attending sports events, "shop 'til you drop" marathons, watching movies—just to name a few. Some people actually pursue having fun with the same seriousness and fervor as others pursue relationships and careers—even becoming "fun addicts." But there are limits. Sadly, nonstop fun-seekers are being guided by a false assumption: that unlimited fun will bring them lasting happiness. It's just not so.

Some people are even willing to take great risks for that euphoric high or rush that comes from *peak experiences* of all types—from bungee-jumping to fantastic vacations to sky diving to Nobel Prizes to significant career accomplishments to lottery winnings. While wonderful and often magnificently rewarding, it turns out that even these peak moments fade. And, in some cases, focusing on peak experiences may even have a negative effect by making everyday life events seem pale by comparison.

Others believe that a long list of sexual conquests produces happiness. But *sex* is not the same as mutually satisfying intimacy. Sex, even lots of it, may be good exercise and is certainly fun—but in itself it can't create feelings of satisfaction, closeness, and true intimacy. Far too often, the loneliness of the morning after lingers long after the thrill of the night before is gone.

Finally, for better or worse, *food and drugs*—both recreational and medicinal—continue to play a major role in the search for increasing pleasure. People can directly influence how happy they feel—often quite easily and dramatically, even if only for a short time—by choosing to partake of certain substances and experiences that directly affect the brain's chemistry. Many popular foods—sugar, carbohydrates, chocolate, alcohol—and hundreds of mood-altering drugs are used regularly to relieve stress, induce sleep, lift mild depression, fight illness, reduce pain, and create various highs. This is a matter of directly affecting the biology of the brain—using biological shortcuts to happiness—to create artificial highs.

Many of these familiar drugs directly activate the feel-good brain chemicals—called neurotransmitters—mainly serotonin, dopamine, glutamate, and endorphins. In fact, there may be at least two hundred neurotransmitters like these that can affect mood. Some are natural. Some are legal—but addictive. Others are dangerous, illegal, and also addictive. For example, endorphins are neurotransmitters whose levels increase to uplift mood after exercise. Prozac and other anti-depressant medications promote the activity of serotonin and dopamine. Alcohol and nicotine affect both dopamine and endorphin circuits in more roundabout ways. Cocaine and many other popular illegal drugs trigger the release of dopamine to produce a very powerful high. Repeated exposure fools the brain into craving these drugs more than food or even sex—explaining why they are so addictive.

All these types of food and drugs offer often almost instant feelings of pleasure. Verifiable physiological changes occur as people respond to these stimuli and feel happier—but these effects are only short-term. So treasure your pleasures, but do so within limits—knowing that their effects are as perishable as ice cream in the warm sun.

Hedonism

Personifying pleasure seeking taken to the extreme without any limits, *hedonists* believe that happiness is all pleasure and no pain—that the goal of life is to experience a continuous succession of all the pleasures possible—a constant high—while avoiding all pain and all effort. People with this view of how to fill the waking hours of each day pursue a simple and seductive mantra: "If I just can accumulate enough pleasurable or fun or peak or sexual experiences and possessions, I'll be happy for the rest of my life." Bigger TVs and houses, more sex, faster cars, prettier women, younger men, more money and material possessions—this is the hedonic treadmill, hedonism in full cry—and it is never-ending. But, as popular a pastime as it is, hedonism is a no-win game for those who want to live sustainably happier lives.

Doomed to Fail

Even though pleasure certainly does yield temporary happiness, solely seeking pleasure—especially in its extreme form, hedonism—is doomed to fail as a major strategy for long-lasting happiness.

Why doesn't hedonism work as a lasting happiness-producing strategy?

For lots of reasons, really. Many powerful forces are arrayed against this popular but ultimately flawed path. No matter how beguiling an approach it seems to be, these forces virtually guarantee that a strategy of or even an obsession with constant pleasure seeking—hedonism—will never result in lasting happiness.

First, expecting any strategy to maintain a constant high is unrealistic. Even people who feel happy with their life overall still experience sadness, loss, disappointment, and pain and suffering at times. No life is a continuous unbroken stream of joy. And second, pleasure and lasting happiness are really two different feelings. Pleasure, even intense pleasure, is the feeling we feel *during* an act—lasting happiness is deeper and more enduring. The feelings associated with any and all of the pleasures are by definition temporary and quick to fade: when the pleasure ends, the pleasurable feelings end soon after. Every pleasurable feeling is transitory in nature, no matter how intense, so expecting them to last is unrealistic.

Beyond these reasons, the deeper force at work is adaptation. No matter what has induced a pleasure-filled high, as time goes by, humans adapt—becoming accustomed to this new state of affairs and seeing it as just the new normal. The new loses its newness—and we adapt or habituate ourselves to the pleasure. Adaptation is an inviolable neurological fact of life: we are wired to respond to novel events—our neurons fire based on new input. So the more repetitive events are, the less our neurons respond. This special form of adaptation is "hedonic adaptation."

Faced with this adaptation reality, some hedonists dedicate themselves to finding out how to continually sustain their temporary happiness highs after they have adapted to them. To do so, they must try to continually find new sources of pleasure—highs followed by higher highs. But, alas, this approach also has its flaws. Repetition inevitably diminishes the highs. Rapid, repeated indulgence of the same pleasure doesn't produce the same levels of enjoyment: the second drink doesn't taste as great as the first, the second skydive is not as thrilling, the second (or third or fourth) use of any mood-enhancing substance doesn't produce the same feeling. Worse, as hedonists try to continually find higher highs to sustain their feelings, pretty soon the negative effects start coming sooner after the highs. They feel hung-over almost before they stop drinking. So they try to run a little faster to stay ahead of the downs. But no one can outrun the truth that constant repetition guarantees diminishing returns. Even worse, not only do the pleasures fade more quickly, repetition may make it necessary, in the search for unending pleasure, to use more and more of the same experience to achieve the same pleasure. And in the process the craving for the experience increases. Attempts to overcome this feeling by taking another drink or drug the morning after, lead down a well-worn path that societies around the world know all too well—the road to addiction.

And to add insult to injury: as many have learned (often the hard way), not only are the pleasurable feelings often very short-term, they are subject to the inevitable crash that follows each high. Since emotions trigger the opposite emotions—psychologists call this the *opponent-process principle*—a drug-induced rush is followed by a morning-after crash. The high from drinking alcohol fades into a hangover. The lift from chocolate melts into a lowering of energy. The pain of childbirth is followed by the euphoria of the new baby—and the ecstasy of that new baby often triggers postpartum depression. The pain from a hard workout releases an endorphin-induced high feeling—and, ironically, the more pain that is endured, the greater high afterward. But, alas, even these new higher highs also wear off. All pleasure peaks are followed by some level of letdown.

In the final analysis, adaptation and these other forces ensure that pleasure seeking can never lead to lasting happiness. Pleasure needs and desires will always increase, so they can never be satisfied. And if you pursue pleasure without limits, neither can you.

TAKE IT TO THE LIMITS—BUT NOT BEYOND

What to do? Don't allow yourself to get caught up in a life solely devoted to unlimited pleasure seeking. A hedonistic strategy of exclusively seeking pleasure is ultimately a dead end on the road to a lastingly happier life. Tempting as they are, the pleasures are not a viable shortcut to lasting happiness. Remember, short-term feelings of pleasure-driven joy are different from longer-term sustainable happiness. Feeling happier via the pleasures is great in the short run, but a focus on hedonism ultimately fosters feelings of emptiness and even depression—and, especially as you age, the gnawing realization that you are just frittering your life away on fluff.

Dismount from the hedonic treadmill. Seek pleasure—but in moderation. Free up valuable time, money, and energy to allow yourself to gain a renewed focus on and priority for the longer-lasting of the six imperatives. As long as you believe happiness is just one more pleasure or conquest or bigger house or faster car away, you will stay tightly tethered to that treadmill—and lasting happiness will always be just out of reach no matter how fast you run. In contrast, lasting happiness is better derived from many frequent positive experiences than from any one single peak experience, no matter how intense and triumphant. Frequency trumps intensity when it comes to how long happiness lasts.

To keep adaptation at bay, space your pleasurable experiences out over a long enough period of time so that each repetition seems new and fresh. This allows a much longer run of positive feelings from your favorite pleasures. Try to take yourself by surprise. Give yourself—or have people close to you give you—surprise presents of the pleasures—such acts have even been found to be reciprocally contagious. Choose experiences instead of purchases—*doing* instead of *owning*.

Learn new pastimes or hobbies instead of spending time shopping—the brightness of new possessions always pales faster than the buyer imagined or hoped. Strive for a stream of active experiences that force you to apply yourself, your mind, and your talents to them rather than engaging in passive pursuits like TV watching.

By all means, seek pleasures of all types—physical, fun, peak experiences, sex, food and drugs—but do so within limits: the quest for them cannot be your only route to a lastingly happier life. Pleasure is without a doubt one prerequisite for a happy and fulfilling life. In fact, without pleasure, life would be a stream of constant emotional pain precluding any possibility of happiness. And without question, a steady diet of the pleasures *does* make people happier, but only in limited ways and for a limited time. Once these short-term pleasurable feelings end, as they inevitably do, people are often left monetarily poorer, physically less healthy, and emotionally diminished—and with an all-too-accurate sense of having wasted valuable time and energy on pursuits that won't yield a lastingly happier life. No matter which pleasure you choose, there is a price paid—and, in the absence of some limits, it's the penultimate price: an unhappy life.

A final consideration: the relentless pursuit of happiness by chasing pleasure at the expense of the other proven paths may really just be an escape—a refuge from dealing with the reality of pain and suffering in life—and an avoidance of the reality that real life requires *effort* to be meaningful. And although this can be one of many defense mechanisms against the emotional pain of confronting problems, even if it's necessary in the short term, myopically continuing to seek pleasure after pleasure can be unhealthy in the longer term. Seek professional help if you recognize this pattern in yourself.

Make seeking pleasure an essential part of your plan to live a happier life—just not the central part. Humans need, want, and love pleasure, but, as this first imperative points out, pleasure within limits is best.

TRANSITION

Seeking pleasure within limits certainly can induce feelings of happiness—at least in the short term. And, as a result, it has an important role in your journey to a happier life. Everyone wants and needs some pleasure in their life.

But, although essential, seeking pleasure is the supreme self-focus strategy. Bear in mind that one of the keys to the kingdom for lasting and sustainable feelings of happiness is the need to move beyond self-focus (because it provides only brief bursts of happiness) and to become more other-focused (which can yield medium and longer-term feelings of joy).

The Second Imperative: Intentionally Think Happy and The Third Imperative: Intentionally Act Happy can both yield medium-term feelings of happiness. These feelings can last for days and weeks and sometimes months (instead of minutes and hours) while also beginning to help you move from being self-focused to being other-focused.

CHAPTER 7

THE SECOND IMPERATIVE: INTENTIONALLY *THINK* HAPPY

The greatest discovery of my generation is that human beings can alter their lives by altering their attitudes of mind.

—William James, American psychologist, called "The Father of Psychology" (1842–1910)

One of the most significant findings of recent generations is the fact that each of us can affect our life in a positive—or negative—manner by changing our thinking. More consciously focusing our thoughts on topics known to increase happiness—intentionally choosing what we think about—allows us both to rise above our genetic "set range" of happiness potential and to slow the process of adaptation.

The Second Imperative: Intentionally *Think* Happy focuses on seven proven ways to deliberately think your way to feeling happier by consciously controlling what you think about on a daily basis. The benefits from deliberately thinking in more positive ways can sometimes last for days, weeks, and even months—a medium-term duration—if you make this intentional thinking a conscious part of your daily thought processes.

Your challenge, should you choose to accept it, is to begin to make more conscious decisions about what you are thinking about at any given minute of each day. Make sure you are thinking about the positive topics in this imperative on a frequent basis while also deliberately controlling and limiting your negative thoughts. To increase the happiness you feel each day, week, and month from now on, repeatedly foster this deliberate thinking about the positive on a regular basis so that it becomes habitual—something you always do all the time.

THINK HAPPY

Happiness doesn't depend on any external conditions, it is governed by our mental attitude.

—Dale Carnegie, American writer and lecturer
(1888–1955)

Choose to think more positively more frequently—doing so will raise your happiness levels and your achievement levels slightly—but only slightly. What we think and then say—both to ourselves and to others—can, over time and to a limited extent, affect what we believe and how we act. "Saying becomes believing" is the social psychology lingo. The truth is that our thoughts influence not only our feelings and actions but also even our actual physiological reactions—blood pressure, pulse, respiratory rate, and digestion.

Since the human brain—even as wondrously fast as it is—can still process only one thought at a time, you can, if you choose, consciously decide exactly what you will think about at any given moment. Only you can think your thoughts. No one else. Taking personal responsibility for your thoughts and your feelings means you decide what to think about, what to dwell upon, and how to feel about the happenings in your life. No one else can make these decisions about the focus of your thinking. How you choose to think about events in your life—past and present—is totally up to you.

So, beginning today, intentionally increase the frequency with which you think and say to yourself positive, healthy thoughts. Let some sunny thoughts brighten any gloom. Decrease time spent on negative, self-deflating thoughts. Create and employ positive affirmations daily—they work and are easy to use. Affirmations are strong, positive statements repeated to yourself about yourself, stating that something that you want to be true is already true. For example, "I am a happy, loving, caring, and kind person." Expand this process to fill more hours of your life with more positive thinking each day and week and month. Resist any negative thoughts. If they continue to arrive unbidden—like a heavy gray cloud weighing down your mind—immediately and consciously replace each one with a thought that triggers positive feelings and emotions. One of the most amazing things about affirmations is they will work even if you don't yet truly believe them. The "saying becomes believing" axiom swings into action, working for you.

Don't let negative thoughts dominate your thinking—they are genuinely toxic, affecting your immune system and physical health, and can lead to depression. Consciously and actively replace every negative thought with a positive one. Remember, just because you believe something doesn't make it true. Your negative thoughts may or may not be factual—for example, one mistake doesn't make you a loser and one failed relationship doesn't make you unlovable forever and being laid off from your job doesn't mean you'll never work again. By more consciously focusing your thinking in positive ways—"thinking happy"—you can create more frequent positive, healthy feelings of happiness in your life each day—at least in a modest way.

BE OPTIMISTIC

They can because they think they can.

—Virgil, Roman poet (70–19 B.C.), *The Aeneid*

See the proverbial glass of life as half-full—and fight against any tendency to the contrary. Be optimistic and hopeful about yourself and about the future. Optimists are more confident than pessimists—and they perform better, are physically healthier, have stronger immune systems, and actually live longer. Intentionally look on the bright side and keep a positive outlook amid the inevitable highs and lows of life—perseverance is born of an optimistic viewpoint. Expect the best for your future—and feel that, if you plan and work to achieve your goals, you will reach them. Intentionally thinking optimistically and planning for a hopeful, positive future sustains happiness in the present and can motivate a positive, goal-directed life.

Stay steady in the face of life's downs—don't dwell on the bad times even when you hit speed bumps on the road to your future. Live your life on a more even keel. Smooth out your volatile emotional ups and downs. Be unflappable. Know that there will be bad days but that they will pass—they do not define you, nor are they the story of your life. Work on being less affected by others' moods and feelings, particularly those closest to you—

your spouse, children, or manager—but not to the point of being uncaring or insensitive.

Never say "try." Optimists just assume they will succeed. Believe that you're going to do things, not just try to do them. Take charge of your life—it's largely what you make it. When the going gets rough, hang tough and work even harder to succeed. Give yourself the benefit of the doubt. When stressed, trust that you can get through the day. Optimists use proven coping methods such as those described later in this chapter when necessary to handle stress and depression.

Learn to Be More Optimistic

There is considerable evidence that the core of human nature is positive: a basic genetic tendency to optimism may be part of our evolutionary inheritance. This makes sense. An optimistic mind-set would be important in the struggle to obtain the basic necessities for survival—food, shelter, social support, and mating opportunities. But, no matter whether or not you have inherited this tendency to look on the bright side and bounce back from life's stresses, optimism can also be learned.

Adapted from Martin Seligman's work, the following three-step process will help you become a more optimistic person:

Step 1: Take an optimistic view.

Step 2: Dispute, distract, and distance.

Step 3: Fight awfulizing.

Step 1: Take an Optimistic View

Consciously begin to use an optimistic style of explanation.

View bad events as being external (As my grandfather used to say, "Blame it on the war"), temporary ("Things always get better in time"), and limited ("Everything else is OK"). Avoid the pessimistic view that negative events are personal ("It's my fault"), permanent ("This is going to last forever"), and pervasive ("It's going to affect everything I do"). How you choose to explain life's events matters. A positive attitude about life and its possibilities yields far more joy than that of a naysayer. In fact, pessimism may be a common thread in depression, anger, hostility, helplessness, and cynicism—not to mention that pessimists are more prone to illnesses, accidents, and violence.

Step 2: Dispute, Distract, and Distance

Intentionally, actively, and immediately block negative thoughts. Then substitute positive ones. This process is called *disputing* your negative thinking and is a deeper and more lasting remedy for negativism. Employ it each time you think a negative thought. In addition, if necessary, *distract* and then *distance* yourself from your negative thoughts. To distract yourself, intentionally interrupt your negative thinking and force yourself to think of something else—anything at all. Focus on this new thought using all your senses until your negativity abates. Distance yourself from your negative thinking by scheduling a time later to think about your negative thoughts, and if they continue to intrude, write down your most worrisome thoughts so you can vent about and dispose of them at a later time. Often, this conscious effort to stand back and suspend belief is enough to fight the pessimism that threatens.

Effort alert: Please don't underestimate how difficult distancing can be to do: it is often much easier to distance yourself from the unfounded accusations of others than from your own accusations aimed at yourself.

Step 3: Fight Awfulizing

Fight against the natural human tendency to awfulize or catastrophize so you can view things in a less destructive way. Making the best of difficult situations without always just thinking of the worst case is a hallmark of optimistic thinking. To balance the tendency to focus on the "worst case scenario," spend 20 or 30 minutes writing what a snapshot of your ideal life could look like in 5 to 10 years—and then list the long-term goals you need to achieve to make that vision a reality. Dispute any negative or pessimistic thinking that may occur during this process.

Two Cautions About Optimism

First, some people are naturally pessimistic and, for them, being optimistic may not be possible—and may even be counterproductive. Their natural approach of setting low expectations, analyzing worst-case scenarios, and preparing carefully enhances their chances of success. One example is in the profession of law, where pessimism is seen as a plus. Trying to force lawyers to be optimistic may be misguided and even harmful in their profession. Still, while the pessimism that drives prudence is valued professionally, the challenge is to contain this tendency in personal life or run a higher risk of depression and unhappiness.

Second, in your zeal to become more optimistic, beware the pitfalls of going too far and becoming an unrealistic dreamer. Don't deny reality or reject any and all unfavorable information. Be vigilant about risks and threats. Take sensible precautions when appropriate. And take action if necessary when faced with real and risky situations. The feelings of invulnerability and immortality are only a magical cloak that people get to wear for a while in their youth. If unbounded, optimism can create infinite frustrations. If people set unrealistic expectations based on mere dreamery, it is their fault and their frustration alone when life intrudes. True optimists are actually more—not less—realistic. They are also more willing to accept bad news—probably because they believe they can make a difference.

Balanced Thinking Is Best

Stay balanced in your thinking. The truth is that not everything is bright and shiny all the time. But neither is everything dull and cloudy. The recipe for happiness, as for so many other things, requires a balance of the positive and the negative: enough optimism to provide hope, tempered with just enough of a pinch of pessimism to prevent complacency and make it possible to take things seriously when required. Optimism in moderation—being "realistically optimistic"—is the ticket, not blindly being positive at the expense of reality.

Choose to stroll on the sunny side of the thought walkway—to be the optimist. Find the opportunity in the crisis by focusing on the possibilities and not the problems. Avoid negative people and thoughts—intentionally challenge them by consciously replacing them with more positive, optimistic ones.

Spend as much time as you can on these proven techniques to achieve and sustain a more optimistic viewpoint about the happenings in your life. It takes work to make taking the optimistic view a habit, but the more you deliberately practice optimistic thinking, the more natural the process will become. Our world today is terrible and filled with cruel people and horrific acts yet at the same time wonderful and filled with love, compassion, and heroism. It is up to you to decide which truth to place first in your thinking.

Always remember that for those who are successful in these fights against negative thought processes, the benefits are great. Optimists are more successful and more likely to have happy marriages, successful careers, and financial security. By being intentionally more optimistic, you can change your reaction to life's challenges—sometimes in the moment—from dejection and surrender to a more positive and hopeful view of the present and the future.

Dare to dream and hope for the best. As with most things in life, you will usually get what you expect.

AVOID EXCESSIVE SELF-FOCUSED RUMINATION

Part of every misery is . . . the fact that you don't merely suffer but have to keep on thinking about the fact that you suffer.

—C. S. Lewis, British scholar and novelist (1898–1963)

Strive to avoid the excessive self-focused rumination that afflicts so many so often. Rumination is the reflective consideration and pondering all sides of an issue—and is often valuable. But it's easy to go too far. *Excessive rumination* is thinking too much—needlessly, endlessly, and excessively pondering the causes, consequences, and meanings of your character, your feelings, or your problems—especially your problems, past and present—and obsessing over questions like "Why am I so unhappy?" "What's the matter with me?" "What did I do to deserve this?" and "How could I be so stupid?"

Many experts actually teach this process—that, to deal with

problems or when feeling depressed, it is necessary to reflect, be introspective, and try to evaluate your feelings and your situation so that you can gain insight and determine solutions. And this approach can be helpful. But sometimes this constant negative and pessimistic thinking can prove overwhelming—taking over your thoughts unbidden and completely—and often making your sadness more instead of less intense, fostering negative thoughts, impairing your ability to concentrate and solve problems, sapping your motivation, and interfering with your initiative.

Beware particularly of the combination of pessimism and excessive rumination—it can turn toxic, taking a significant toll on your feelings and becoming a barrier to living a happier life. Mulling over bad events, brooding, and thinking excessively about bad things can be especially damaging for a pessimistic person and can lead to lowered expectations and feelings of failure that, if left unaddressed, can actually cause clinical depression.

Break the habit of excessive rumination. If any portion of this discussion strikes a chord, begin to work immediately to deliberately change your thinking process. Distract yourself by engaging in activities that divert your energy and attention from the darkness of excessive brooding. Take time to lose yourself in some activity you enjoy that is absorbing and grabs your full attention—to grasp a moment's respite from being held captive by your negative thoughts.

Better yet, consciously redirect your thoughts into more neutral or even optimistic ones by first telling yourself to *stop* your negative thoughts. If you need to, actually say it out loud: *"Stop."* In extreme cases, some people wear a rubber band around their wrist and snap it to remind them to stop excessive ruminating.

Once you've successfully redirected your attention away

from negative rumination, follow the same process you used when dealing with pessimistic thoughts: distance yourself from your brooding by writing down your ruminations now to temporarily dispose of them and then schedule a specific time so you can deal with them later. Writing your negative thoughts down lessens their strength and their hold on your thought processes now and in the interim until you come back to them. This kind of respite tends to lessen their import and tone their impact down to more manageable levels.

Implement these techniques—they can enable even the most diligent of excessive ruminators to break the iron grip on their thought processes and outlook on life. They can free your energy and time to intentionally focus your thinking on the positive goal of living a happier life.

BUILD RESILIENCE

> *Our greatest glory is not in never falling, but in rising every time we fall.*
>
> —Confucius, Chinese philosopher and teacher
> (557? —479 B.C.)

Choose to intentionally think in ways that build resilience—it is a proven path to a happier life. *Resilience* is the innate capability to bounce back from adversity—to cope with, adapt to, survive, and even thrive in the face of the ongoing and inevitable stresses, challenges, drama and trauma, tragedy, and even catastrophes life brings. Resilience helps you avoid becoming a victim—stuck in a position of long-lasting helplessness—and also to avoid the pain that accompanies that role. Resilience is not just toughing it out or ignoring feelings of loss and sorrow; it does not require becoming emotionally distant, cold, or unfeeling, nor does it mean going it alone. In fact, reaching out for social support is one of the hallmarks of being resilient.

Some people can start over and create a whole new life after a horrific calamity—like losing everything to a tornado or a tsunami—while others are defeated by the smallest of setbacks. Resilient people refuse to dwell on the loss. Instead, they choose to deal with it, adapt, and learn from the experience. They are even able to remain generally optimistic as they rebound from whatever the setback is—and usually they rebound relatively quickly. The resilient may be scarred, but they adapt and continue on in the other domains of their life without self-destructive behaviors.

To build resiliency, don't isolate yourself. Share the trauma you are facing with close loved ones—family and friends—who can listen to you and offer support. Stay connected—seeking help can sustain you in difficult times. Recall how you've coped with challenges in the past and use that insight to take action—both to address the trauma and to cope with your feelings. Don't just wish your problems would go away. Figure out what you need to do, make a plan, and begin to act. Doing something—however small—toward solving the problem every day gives you a sense of control—of accomplishment—in dealing with the events and situations in your life.

Be proud of yourself for taking action—and use that sense of pride to motivate you to continue. Stay positive and trust yourself to make sound decisions to address your challenges. You can't change what has happened, but you can remain hopeful and optimistic about the future—even if you can only catch an occasional glimpse of how things might improve. Look for positive progress every day. Remaining positive about the future—and even finding humor in distressing and stressful situations—isn't a sign of denial; rather, it is a helpful coping mechanism. Macabre humor has lightened many a life-threatening situation. Through it all, find time and energy to take care of yourself. Tend to your own physical and emotional needs. Keep participating in activities you enjoy, exercise regularly, and sleep and eat well. Try to enlarge your perspective to both see your challenge in the larger context of your life and the world at large and even to find some positive meaning in the trauma that is engulfing you. Ask yourself: will this matter in a year? Or in five? Regardless of the slight or setback, consider using forgiveness as a strategy to compartmentalize the immediate trauma and limit its effect on the remainder of your life—both today and in the future. Search for something in the situation to be grateful for—even if it is only gratitude that you have the capability to handle it. Resilience is real but not inevitable. Persistence, hardiness, a motivation toward goals and achievement, and an optimistic outlook are all traits associated with greater resilience.

Strive to be a resilient survivor, not a victim. So often, our ability to handle the inevitable opportunities life deals out is quite astounding. First, we do everything we can to avoid difficulties and hardships. Then, when they happen, we doubt we can get through them. Yet, even after all that, when faced with them, most of us are able to reach down and find the inner strength to deal with them and eventually even run toward the light at the end of the tunnel—without thinking about oncoming trains. Think of resiliency as "emotional buoyancy"—something to help you stay afloat and survive amid a churning sea of hardship and chaos—and build it into every fiber of your being.

SAVOR THE PAST, PRESENT, AND FUTURE

We often live life as if the present were merely our means to the future.

— Blaise Pascal, French mathematician and philosopher
(1623–1662)

Nurture the habit of intentionally taking time to savor the past, the present, and the future—allowing frequent and often intense thoughts of remembered past, current present, and potential future happiness to flood you with positive feelings. Omitting the myriad references to taste and smell, *to savor* means "to enjoy with appreciation, to relish." Savoring is a powerful, intentional thought process that lets you deliberately bring remembered and imagined feelings of happiness right into the present moment to delight in and take pleasure from whenever you'd like to do so.

Savor the past by *reminiscing*, the present by being more present—more *mindful*—in each moment, and the future by *fantasizing* about upcoming positive events.

Reminiscing

Reminisce on a regular basis—either alone or with others who share the memories. Mutual reminiscence—sharing memories with other people—yields abundant positive emotions. This is particularly true for the more mature among us, as the years fill a treasure chest full of life experiences to draw upon for pleasant memories. Listen to your favorite music from your past. Take a mental pilgrimage to meaningful places from your past. Memory-build by taking mental photographs of an experience, and then reminisce about it later with others. Often, our memories are all we have left of those lost to us.

Nurture your ability to be nostalgic on a regular basis—it will allow you to reconnect with your cherished memories of beauty, pleasure, goodness, and love. Enjoy moments of self-congratulation by reminding yourself how impressed others are or were and recall how long you waited for this event or that accomplishment to happen. Repetitively replay your happiest days—those moments in your life that were peaks of pleasure. Often, they are the "firsts" in all life domains—first kiss, first love, first graduation, first marriage, first childbirth, first day on your first job, first award, first sunset, first divorce, and so on. Don't analyze these events, just replay and revel in your memories of them.

Don't shy away from remembrance of the bittersweet memories—they too have their place. By only recalling the greatest highs, you risk discontent with your present. Better to recall that, in truth, everything is transient. By acknowledging that all positive (and negative) moments in your past eventually ended, you may be more motivated to seize the moment and enjoy the present. Nostalgia can be triggered spontaneously by chance or intentionally by deliberate, active reflection. Group all your photos of your favorite people, places, memories, and things into a "savoring album"—and revel in the mental photographs of your best memories. Take time to look at the album on a regular basis—but not too frequently. Choose to spend time in active reflections on your past pleasures. Notice that the more you reminisce about the past, the more pleasure you feel from the savoring of the memory and the better you can enjoy the present. If you master this, no matter what happens, "you'll always have Paris."

Mindfulness

Strive to savor and enjoy more things as they happen—to live more in the moment—but without overdoing it. This is often called "being more mindful" or "mindful awareness" or simply "mindfulness." It is a form of right-now meditation designed to slow down your thoughts and help you focus on the immediate present moment—as distinguished from future-mindedness.

Although some would argue its scientific impossibility, try to savor the now—since it's really all any of us have—and stay in the present moment. Enjoy the positive experiences and moments in your life more fully as they occur. Block out thoughts of other things you should be doing, wondering what comes next, or determining how the event could be improved. Just *be*. Too often, we spend our lives so focused on tomorrow that we miss the happiness in today.

Reflect on and relish some current, ordinary moments daily for two or three minutes each. It is often these little things in a day that turn out to be the big things. Staying in the moment longer can both produce pleasure in the present and limit anxiety about the uncertainties of the future. Hone your appreciation of beauty in nature and humans. Admire talent, genius, virtue, and excellence in all endeavors. Begin to notice and appreciate and take pleasure in the most mundane, everyday experiences. Stay absorbed in each moment longer than normal by using all your senses to focus your attention. Try not to think of anything else—just marvel by losing yourself in the moment and make it precious. Although it may be difficult at first, if you can, just sense, don't think. When you finish a task, bask in the accomplishment for a few moments. To help you, employ your camera or phone in a special way that allows you to truly focus on a specific moment. By trying to only take the perfect picture of the perfect moment, you can become more mindful and more appreciative and enjoy each experience more—both now in the present and as a reminder of the past. Choose to share a savoring moment with family or a friend who similarly values an experience—sharing can heighten the pleasures of savoring. Share with them and tell them how much you value the moment.

Pausing to enjoy the present moment—being more mindful—is, in a way, a form of gratitude. It will keep you appreciative of all the great things you have now—instead of being focused on what you lack—and can act as an antidote to constant upward comparison. When practiced regularly, mindfulness can be a powerful tool to increase feelings of happiness on a daily basis.

Fantasizing

Fantasize about your ideal future. Picture in your mind's eye every detail of the life you will realize when you accomplish your most precious life goals—a marriage, a job, the peak of your career, a new home, a special vacation, a new baby, a golden retirement. Allow yourself uninterrupted time to visualize the details of what these experiences will look like and how you'll feel at that moment. Bringing these "memories of the future" back to enjoy in the present heightens your pleasure now—and can brighten your mood during the inevitable less-happy times to come.

A caution. Like everything, savoring can be overdone. A balanced life includes learning from the errors of the past, savoring the present moments, and planning for a realistic future. Seek to strike a balance in your intentional thinking between savoring your past and present special moments and your visions for the future—while at the same time taking the necessary actions to make your present a success and those future visions a reality.

A FINAL WORD

Savoring is a new field that makes it possible to reclaim some of the lost opportunity of the present. Although seemingly a simple task, savoring takes some motivation and effort. It requires redirecting your mind from its everyday focus on the tasks at hand—at best a daunting prospect in the 24/7 world of today. To optimize the feelings of happiness to be gained from savoring in all three time dimensions, use your willpower to make it a habit now—and almost second nature soon. If you persevere, by becoming aware of the pleasure you get from the deliberate conscious attention to past memories, more mindfulness of the present moment, and vivid fantasies about a positive future, you can enjoy them all in the present—and you will feel happier for the effort.

DEVELOP HEALTHY SELF-ESTEEM

Self-esteem isn't everything; it's just that there's nothing without it.

— Gloria Steinem, American feminist, journalist, and social and political activist (1934-)

Value and nurture healthy self-esteem—it is a powerful ally in the lifelong pursuit of happiness and fulfillment. Healthy self-esteem—positive, yet based on genuine achievement of realistic goals—is a critical part of healthy development and provides a sturdy foundation for enduring joy. Within limits, those with strong feelings of self-worth persevere when the going gets tough, regain their confidence more easily when faced with traumatic life events, are less vulnerable to illnesses and drug abuse, and cope with life's inevitable challenges, stresses, and uncertainties in healthier ways. Satisfaction with self—a feeling of being accepted for who one is—is a major contributor in all corners of the world to satisfaction with life in general. Although not as large a benefit as once hoped, high self-esteem has two clear benefits: increased happiness and enhanced initiative.

How to Develop It

Accomplish something. Bolster self-esteem by the genuine achievement of realistic goals—within the confines of your individual limitations. Define and then dedicate yourself to pursuing a life-changing goal. Take on multiple roles that offer a sense of autonomy or engage in a new, stimulating challenge that is doable. Surmounting challenges and taking on new roles allow you to expand your identity, which increases your self-confidence and provides an alternative source of self-esteem: now you can be a [spouse] and a [parent] and [a success in your chosen work] and have [a hobby or interest you enjoy]—and these multiple roles can enhance your ability to be comfortable with and proud of the person you've become.

When necessary, rise to the challenge and overcome the trauma in life—a courageous response to a crisis can lead to higher self-esteem and a new self-perception of added competence. Value those skills and tasks in which you excel—savor the feelings of mastery as you perform at your peak. Express gratitude more frequently—be grateful for both how much you have accomplished and how much support you've received from other people. Gratitude fights negative thinking about failures and disappointments, which can diminish your view of yourself. Learn to forgive—forgiveness takes a big person.

Engage in nostalgic remembrances—they allow you to relive the moments when you were the star in your own play—and you will feel better about yourself as a result.

Strive to create an internal, self-rewarding system that lets you feel good when you've tried hard and done the best you can—no matter what the outcome. For some, this is an innate ability while others seem to find it more of a challenge to do successfully. Exercise regularly—doing good things for yourself increases self-esteem and reduces depression. Meditate—calm allows you to be more accepting of life and self. Seek a quiet, secure confidence in yourself. Avoid arrogance or cockiness—these are unattractive and the preserve of the small and the insecure. Be comfortable saying to yourself "I'm OK"—but be sure this positive self-view is based on genuine accomplishment of realistic goals. If a believer, foster your relationship with God—it can allow you to feel unconditionally valued, loved, and cared for and thus provide you with a sense of security and self-worth.

Without engaging in self-flagellation, gain self-knowledge via an honest self-appraisal of your capabilities and shortcomings. Having a realistic and accurate self-image leads to self-liking and more self-confidence. Combat any negative images that aren't founded in reality. Take a firm and immediate stand against self-hate in any form—thought or verbal or physical. Pry away any and all "emotional vampires"—they can suck the happiness right out of anyone. Curtail time spent with people—including relatives—who do nothing but complain and are critical and not supportive of your aspirations and dreams. If your vampire is a spouse or significant other, try counseling. Within limits and without denying obvious issues, believe and repeat, "I can't be responsible for what others think." There will always be some people who disapprove of something you say or do.

For children in your care, realistically assess the child's abilities and give unconditional parental love—but not indiscriminate and unconditional approval, praise, or rewards. Instead, give deserved recognition for a job well done. Approve behavior you want to see more of and ignore or punish behavior you want to see less of. Be careful to recognize and reward honest effort to meet a reasonable set of standards, allowing for the fact that everyone has different strengths and weaknesses. Emphasize strengths and specific skills and encourage feelings of competence instead of offering the "everything you do is great" sort of empty praise. For children who are acting up and not working hard, don't praise them to get them to feel good about themselves so they will try harder—that is a flawed approach. Instead, give them a reality check and let them know they will be praised when they do something that is praiseworthy. Teach children the tools necessary for real self-confidence: accomplishment, perseverance, integrity, and the willingness to work hard.

Help others—as noted earlier, moving beyond self-focus will elevate your feelings about yourself. And, while helping others, ensure that praise you give is sincere and is tied to real accomplishment, performance, and behavior. The real worry is people who have an inflated sense of self that has no basis in reality.

The Great Barrier Warning

In the end, a balanced view of self is best. Healthy self-esteem is better than self-esteem that is either too high, phony and unwarranted, or unrealistically low. In particular, be wary of these barriers to healthy self-esteem—they are powerful and ubiquitous:

Phony, high self-esteem brought about by empty praise. Severe disappointment awaits when schools and employers don't agree that someone is special just because they showed up. Unrealistic and unwarranted self-esteem often leads to narcissism—total self-absorption resulting in a sense of entitlement and a selfish worldview. Narcissists expect praise and adulation regardless of their behavior or performance. As children, they often respond to criticism from parents or teachers by saying, "Well, *I* think it's fine." An inflated self-view can continually subject a person to disappointment, frustration, depression, and even rage when reality intrudes and the world does not validate an idealized, inflated, or unwarranted self-image.

Unrealistically low self-esteem. Conversely—and just as damaging—if self-esteem is too low, people can't take credit for the good things they do and build up their confidence appropriately, because they don't believe they deserve it. Women in particular often take everything personally and ascribe any good performance to luck. Feelings of inferiority can be fanned by constant unfavorable upward comparisons. Unless counterbalanced by downward comparisons and a reality check, these feelings can lead to lowered self-esteem, unhappiness, despair and even depression. When people's—even relatively accomplished people's—self-esteem is threatened, they become defensive, inflate their own accomplishments, denigrate others, exhibit increased hostility, judge others more harshly, and disparage more. People who feel or who are made to feel insecure or unworthy will often try to reestablish their self-worth by putting others down.

If any of these barriers describe your approach to the world, remember that traditional psychology often traces self-esteem issues to early upbringing. Consider trying psychotherapy to investigate the historic causes of these issues. Any improvement will be a boon to your pursuit of a happier life.

Why It Matters

The importance of self-esteem to happiness cannot be overestimated. Implementing any or all of the techniques described here for increasing legitimate self-esteem is critical: satisfaction with self is one of the more important contributors to satisfaction with life in general. More specifically, to pursue a happier life, you need to feel some sense of inherent worthiness—to be worthy of the pursuit. If you feel you don't deserve happiness, you will act in ways that make it a self-fulfilling prophecy: your feelings of being unworthy of happiness in fact lead to unhappiness. When you deny your inherent worth—or, worse, work to actively undermine your self-belief by refusing to accept good things that happen to you—you undermine your talents, your accomplishments, your potential—risking chronic unhappiness. As a colleague's philosophy professor once said, "It's easy to underestimate the damage you can do to your own soul."

Remember: your own thoughts and beliefs are powerful. Earn healthy self-esteem by accomplishment and performance and behavior. Then, allow that feeling of inner worth to help you navigate life's storms with some serenity, secure in the knowledge that you are worthy of a happier life and are willing to work to achieve it.

TAKE CONTROL

Hell is to drift, heaven is to steer.

—George Bernard Shaw, Nobel Prize–winning Irish dramatist and critic (1856–1950), *Don Juan in Hell*

Intentionally take control and make decisions in your own life—acting on your life is what provides that delicious feeling of being in control of your destiny. Even though, in its largest sense, absolute control is an illusion, one major happiness-producer is still to feel some sense of control over your life, over yourself, over your expectations, over coping with hardship and pursuing your goals. Simply put: the more in control you feel, the happier you are. Take control over your life in the following ways:

- Exert personal control
- Improve self-control
- Manage expectations
- Master major coping strategies
- Commit to goals

Exert Personal Control

Short of being obsessively and compulsively controlling, exert a strong sense of personal control over your life when circumstances allow. Autonomy leads to higher morale and health, higher achievement in school and at work, and better coping with stress as well as a happier life. Choose your destiny to the extent possible in your individual circumstances. And choose carefully: life exacts a price for every decision. Nurture an internal locus of control—a belief that, within limits, the direction of your future and what happens to you in your life is largely your own doing. It is the feeling of influencing events in life that matters when it comes to happiness, and even good fortune or fate taking a hand—winning the lottery or dodging an accident—can cause distress by serving as a reminder that control is an illusion and we are really all just pawns in our own life play.

Beyond these life-influencing efforts, manage your personal time effectively. Strive for a healthy balance in your use of time—unoccupied, unfilled, open, and uncommitted time is a recipe for unhappiness. Too often people in modern Western societies fill too much of their time with empty activities—sleeping late, hanging out, excessive TV watching—all of which leave the unhappy, hollow feeling of a lack of accomplishment. Better to fill your time by creating your plans and backing them up with detailed to-do lists and deadlines. Schedule your daily activities to support those plans—and then, as you finish them, check off each item on your to-do list as complete. Enjoy the positive feeling of personal control that you get each and every time you meet a deadline, no matter how small it may be. The sense of mastery you feel by directing and personally controlling events in your life will contribute to your happiness—sometimes even more than the events themselves.

Improve Self-Control

Work at being better able to control your emotions. Strive to hold your desires, needs, and impulses in check as appropriate for each situation—just knowing how to behave is not enough. Learn to self-regulate your emotions and your reactions when the inevitable negative events happen in life. Try to neutralize your negative feelings on your own—and then repair them if you still hurt. Strive to remain cheerful even in the most trying of situations. In times of stress or anger, take a deep breath before speaking. If angry, resist the urge to retaliate by being critical, negative, or sarcastic—learn to think through your feelings of anger. Fight against uncontrolled displays of your true human primitive nature—but also accept its inevitability: short of genetic intervention, we humans can only be who we are. Model disciplined self-control of emotions. Learn to postpone immediate gratification of wants and appetites if necessary. Instead, be temperate—wait for appropriate opportunities to satisfy your desires in more moderate ways so that no harm is done to yourself or others. Make a healthy effort to improve—but also strive to accept yourself for who you are, allowing some calm and peace into your life.

Manage Expectations

Strive to manage and sometimes restrain your expectations to gain more control over your life. Let go of unrealistic and impossible expectations for happiness, for success, for your children, for your career, for your relationships, for your life. Don't expect to be happy all the time or to achieve perfection in everything, Even though striving for perfection must be the standard, like it or not, imperfection rules. Nothing and no one is perfect. Face up to this truth—or risk continually setting unrealistic expectations that can jeopardize your happiness. Make your expectations and aspirations more realistic by redefining what would be a meaningful achievement given a realistic assessment of your life, your capabilities, and your situation.

Strike a balance between taking control to make life go your way and accepting and making do with what life has to offer. Highs and lows are a part of every life, as are beginnings and endings—both are as inevitable as sunrises and sunsets. Life is truly not fair, nor is it simple. Instead, unfairness, uncertainty, and complexity are the norm. Like it or not, this is an impermanent world. Everything—the good and even the terrible—changes. Yet, at the same time, don't let managing your expectations blind you to the reality that life's greatest achievements and greatest disappointments both stem from the highest of expectations.

Part of growing up means readjusting expectations and accepting that some wishes and goals and desires just can't be fulfilled. Few of us will ever see our own face carved onto Mt. Rushmore, or even on a hometown statue. But, from this realization, we gain the wisdom and perspective to achieve our goals within the limitations imposed by the realities of life— our limited choices, our diminishing capabilities as we age, and our imperfect connections even with our loved ones. At a certain point, each of us is likely to find it necessary to lower our unrealistic aspirations and expectations to more reality-based levels. Life unmasks us all. So adjust your expectations, especially as you age. Things don't always get better. Exorbitant, unrealistic expectations will more often than not doom you to perpetual frustration, disappointment, disillusionment, and ultimate unhappiness.

Master Major Coping Strategies

Master the major strategies needed to cope with the inevitable loss, challenges, hardship, trauma, and pain and suffering that are the realities of life. Everybody hurts—sometime. Coping is the first step to regain some measure of control over the random and often chaotic happenings that are the norm in all of our lives. Applying proven coping strategies can relieve the stress and the pain and suffering from these negative life events and situations.

Immediately move into problem-solving mode for challenges where it looks like something constructive can be done to actually fix the situation. Become Mr. or Ms. Fix-it. Applying problem-solving coping can not only sometimes solve the immediate problem but it can also reduce depression by taking control of the situation.

There are, however, some problems and situations that just can't be fixed: the loss of a relationship, the end of a good job, the death of a loved one, for example. There are also other times when negative emotions are so overwhelming that it's impossible to take action to solve the problem. Here, the best you can do is to deal constructively with your emotions by implementing some blend of the following coping strategies:

- Allow time to pass—even just 24 hours can improve your ability to cope.

- No matter what has happened, view the loss and the pain just as "It's my turn"—and know that everyone gets a turn at one time or another.

- Take the long view: almost all immediate, overwhelming life crises will, one day in the future, be viewed as "Wow, remember that tough patch I went through back then"—just a normal part of life's inevitable peaks and valleys.

- Compartmentalize by distinguishing between your feelings about the loss and your normal life—so you can keep functioning while you recover emotionally.

- Distract yourself with exercise.

- Even if you don't feel like it, engage in pleasurable activities. Do something that you enjoy to give yourself a respite from your emotions until time passes and you are better equipped to deal with the problem.

- Seek comfort and emotional social support from people close to you.

- If a believer, turn to religion to find solace in spiritual beliefs, including a belief in the afterlife, and to get support from God and the religious community.

- Try to reinterpret the situation to see if you can learn from the experience—to find some meaning or something good in what has happened—often talking or writing can help you rethink your views about life including its inevitable last phase, death.

And, ultimately, after some varying length of time, reach acceptance and learn to live with the reality of what has happened—and possibly move beyond to achieve personal growth—to create something of value or even flourish in the aftermath of the trauma or loss. Maybe you can even gain a chance for redemption if needed. Through it all, be gentle with yourself—some things are unknowable. Take comfort from the truth that there is no higher order of existence humans need to aspire to. Facing our own mortality—as we each must do one day—reminds us that, ultimately, each of us is alone in a fundamental way anyway. Mastering these major coping tools is critical for our well-being—for there are no limits to losses in life.

Commit to Goals

Passionately commit to setting and then achieving your goals. Deciding to pursue your bliss says you have some level of control over the direction your life is traveling. Just setting goals communicates that you have confidence in yourself and believe you are capable of overcoming whatever obstacles you face to achieve them—that you can be the active architect of your future instead of merely a passive bystander bouncing along at the whim of the waves in your life. Without goals and efforts to pursue them, you risk being consumed by the emptiness and agony of an aimless and self-absorbed life. Choose your major life goals wisely. Commit to those that are truly important, that have intrinsic value, resonate with your deeply held values, provide enjoyment and meaning, and are involving and rewarding—and then prioritize your life around them.

Goals you *want* to achieve can inspire you to greatness and lastingly increase your level of happiness—unlike those you are required to achieve or that have been chosen for you by others. Choose goals that are appropriate for your stage of life—that reflect the authentic you and any legacy you wish to leave for your family or society. And select goals that are uniquely yours: the ruts from the past are always deep.

Ironically, taking action to achieve goals other than happiness is a proven path to achieving your goal of feeling happier. Committing to goals satisfies your need for autonomy—to be in control of your decisions and behavior and to feel a sense of competence in dealing with the world around you. People who set goals and strive to achieve something that is personally significant to them—something that has intrinsic value to them—are far happier than those who don't have strong dreams or aspirations. Mapping your course and then following your dreams is a proven path to a sustainably happier life.

Remember that no road to a better future is without its twists and turns, so be flexible and willing to adapt as situations change. Always keep your ultimate goal in mind—there are usually multiple routes through the forest. Put your best plans in place—but also plan to be surprised: life (and love too, for that matter) is often a mess and a muddle. Simplify your life by eliminating nonessential goals, goals that are less important. Work hard and make progress to achieve your goals—pursuing goals not only makes people happier but negates fear and can even stave off depression. Often, as much happiness lies in the striving to reach goals as in their accomplishment.

TAKING CONTROL COUNTS

More fully adopt these various ways of thinking—and regain some sense of control over your life. No matter whether this increased sense of control is gained by exerting better personal control over your life, yourself, and your emotions, by managing your expectations more deliberately, by mastering major coping strategies to deal with hardship and stress, or by committing more fully to your goals, taking control over your life can reliably increase the level of happiness possible for you.

TRANSITION

Intentionally manage your thinking by incorporating the seven strategies of The Second Imperative: Intentionally Think Happy *into your daily life. Although thinking happy, being optimistic, avoiding excessive self-focused rumination, building resilience, savoring the past, present, and future, developing healthy self-esteem, and taking control of various aspects of your thinking take conscious effort on a daily—or even a minute-by-minute or hour-by-hour—basis, they are worthwhile—and every worthwhile change requires focus and energy. Incorporate these strategies to increase the number and quality of positive thoughts in your daily life, and you'll find that they can reliably and sustainably lift your spirits every day. And, with some diligence and perseverance, by thinking happier every day, you can make your life over the medium term of days, weeks, and even months begin to be measurably happier.*

Although still mostly self-focused on your own thinking, the proven strategies in The Second Imperative: Intentionally Think Happy*—when implemented into your life—can provide you with a tremendous amount of positive feeling.*

However, not only can you think *your way to a happier life, you can* act *your way there also.*

In The Third Imperative: Intentionally Act Happy*, the focus shifts outward. The strategies and actions in this next imperative will positively affect those around you and, as a result of affecting others, you will find that you too can feel frequent positive bursts of happiness in the medium term—often lasting for days, weeks, or months, and sometimes even longer.*

CHAPTER 8

THE THIRD IMPERATIVE: INTENTIONALLY *ACT* HAPPY

Act as if you were already happy and that will tend to make you happier.

— Dale Carnegie, American writer and lecturer
(1888–1955)

Begin to deliberately *act* more frequently in planned and intentional ways that are known to increase your feelings of happiness. Consciously acting in certain proven ways works because our attitudes follow our behavior. In fact, one of social psychology's arch principles states that people are just as likely to *act* themselves into new ways of thinking as they are to *think* themselves into new ways of acting. Simply acting like a happy person has been proven by decades of research to increase the happiness actually felt—at least at a modest level of intensity.

The Third Imperative: Intentionally *Act* Happy puts this "attitudes follow behavior" principle to work for you. Your challenge is to learn, understand, and then implement into your life the ways of intentionally acting that are known to increase happiness. Instead of resigning yourself to your current set of behavior traits and emotions, you can stretch yourself beyond them and actually *act* yourself into new ways of thinking. Intentional positive acts breed new attitudes and new positive beliefs—usually about yourself—which trigger positive emotions so you feel happier. As the leading actor in your own life play, playing these new roles can uplift your mood in an ever-upward spiral. For example, smiling makes you feel a little happier; frowning makes you feel a little angry. Even if you're in a bad mood, talking with a friend can leave you feeling better and less upset—regardless of anything the friend says. Acting as if you are kind, thoughtful, caring, and sensitive boosts your sense of self-esteem. Pretending to be more outgoing makes you somewhat more so. And, over time, acting-as-if becomes believing. Role-playing becomes reality. Just as playing the role of a parent, over time, becomes the real thing, if you act happier and kinder, or more forgiving and more grateful, or more outgoing, after a while, that is what you will be. Said another way, your inward dispositions follow your outward actions of what you desire to be.

The impact of these new behaviors can be significant. As with thinking yourself happy, acting yourself happy uplifts your levels of happiness for far longer than simply seeking pleasure. While not an overnight attitude adjustment, acting in certain proven ways can—over time—lead to medium-term feelings of happiness—lasting days, weeks, and months. These longer intervals of feeling happier provide you with a major clue about how to reprioritize and spend the limited time you have each day so as to optimize the happiness you can experience in your life.

ACT HAPPY

We shall never know all the good things that a simple smile can do.

— Mother Teresa, Nobel Peace Prize winner
(1910–1997)

Intentionally act as if you are happy by smiling, by laughing, by acting engaged in conversations and in life in general as well as by mimicking the energy and enthusiasm of happy people. And do this more frequently. Acting in these ways not only allows you to receive the same benefits that happy people receive—returned smiles, stronger friendships, and more success at school or work—it can actually make you feel happier.

Smile

Make it a habit to smile more frequently each day—except, of course, when inappropriate. Smile regularly even when you might be feeling uncertain or down. The simple act of smiling—and smiling in a hearty way with cheeks raised— can buoy up your mood and your entire being. Happy people smile more than others. And, when you smile, smile with your eyes by contracting the muscles around them (called the *orbicularis oculi*), not just with your mouth muscles. This is called the *Duchenne smile* (after the eighteenth-century French physiologist who first described it) and it signals genuine joy—as opposed to the "flight attendant" smile, which is polite but less than sincere. Remember, there is truth in the adage: smile and the world really does smile with you.

Try this strategy today and observe other people responding more positively by smiling back, initiating conversations, engaging with or helping or comforting you more readily. If you're a new mother, smile and your infant will respond in kind. People will light up just by feeling the warmth of your smile. Try it and see. And remember the benefits: people with Duchenne smiles turn out to be happier people; they get married earlier, are happier in marriage, and feel less stress and more well-being.

Laugh

Laugh more often—it is another behavior of happy people. If the smile is a subtle signal of a happy person, then laughter is a major social signpost. Seek more opportunities, friends, and situations that make you laugh—laughter is 30 times as frequent in social situations as when you're alone. If meeting in person isn't convenient, reach out regularly to call special friends. Since laughter is infectious (recall sitcom sound tracks?) and often a two-way pleasure street, reciprocal laughter from the listener is often an instant reward for you. And don't just laugh: if appropriate, laugh vigorously—vigorous laughter seems to be good for your health by exercising your heart and boosting your mood. Even the anticipation of laughter can cause positive changes in your body.

Imitate

Act happy by imitating the various facial expressions and postures of happy people. In addition to smiling and laughing, stand up tall more frequently. Walk confidently more often with longer, purposeful strides. Act livelier and more enthusiastic. Actively listen and be more engaged in conversations. If you're feeling down, feign cheerfulness when talking with a friend. Hug others more frequently—when appropriate. And look for reciprocity—other people will unconsciously begin to mimic your face, posture, and voice when you are acting in happy ways—we all do it.

Stretch Yourself . . .

While it is unrealistic to expect these new ways of acting happy to result in your feeling more upbeat overnight, if you stretch yourself one day at a time—even if at first you don't feel like it—to go through the outward motions and act happy, smile and laugh more, and simulate outgoingness—you will become more so and these actions will trigger your positive emotions. Even mild positive feelings can begin an upward spiral of improved consequences benefiting you and those closest to you, making it easier for you to cope by reducing the anxiety and distress you feel and gradually allowing you to realize greater and greater levels of joy. Trust the "attitude follows behavior" principle. Even these relatively simple positive behaviors can begin to reshape your self-view—and you really can begin to feel at least modestly happier each day from now on.

. . . And Others

And there are added benefits. Acting happy not only lets *you* feel happier, but it can also spread happy feelings throughout your social network—perhaps because other people copy the facial expressions and bodily actions seen in happy people. The concept of emotional contagion has shown that emotional states can transfer from one person to another. Said another way, people can "catch" others' emotional feelings—not only happiness, but also anger and mild depression. This neatly explains why it's fun to be around happy people and depressing to be around those who are depressed. Parenthetically, sadness and unhappiness can also spread throughout social networks—but, fortunately for everyone, not as efficiently.

So, while acting happy can increase your happiness, amazingly, you can also spread your happiness to your social network *and* your happiness can also increase because of the happiness of those around you. Recent studies have shown that, incredibly, happiness is *contagious*. In fact, feelings of happiness can spread throughout a social network for up to three degrees of separation—to people who don't even know one another. In the same way obesity and the likelihood of quitting smoking have been shown to spread through social groups, the happiness of friends, spouses, siblings, or neighbors all living within one mile increases the probability that you will be happy by up to 15 percent and can last as long as one year. As the Buddha said, "Thousands of candles can be lit from a single candle, and the life of the candle will not be shortened. Happiness never decreases by being shared." Amazing, yet maybe just common sense when you think about the concept of emotional contagion as also being a collective phenomenon.

EXPRESS GRATITUDE

Gratitude is the secret to life.

—Albert Schweitzer, Nobel Prize–winning German/French physician and philosopher (1875–1965)

Intentionally express gratitude in specific, proven ways more frequently—it is a reliable path to increase your feelings of happiness by up to 25 percent—and these happier feelings can last for as long as six months.

Long extolled by philosophers and spiritual teachers ranging from Cicero to Buddha, by priests, pastors, and religious leaders around the world, and even by most parents, gratitude has been and continues to be many things to many people. It can be an internal feeling of wonder, thankfulness, and appreciation for life in general or for your own life in particular. It can be a matter of seeing the bright side—viewing life as abundant, not taking things for granted, literally counting your blessings. And it can also be saying thank you to others, and, for believers, thanking God. Gratitude in all its forms has long been prized as a morally positive emotion that encourages reciprocal kindness.

And positive psychologists have now reinforced its value: expressing gratitude, independent of any faith or religious affiliation or lack thereof, has been observed to increase feelings of happiness, pride, hope, excitement, and joy, and to increase social ties and defy depression. Gratitude is the antidote to envy and jealousy. Being grateful for what you have allows you some serenity, thwarts unfavorable upward comparisons, and makes it less likely that you will pay attention to what the Joneses may have that you don't. Because of this, gratitude may actually deter and even diminish anger, bitterness, and greed—they seem to shrink when face-to-face with gratitude.

Following are the major proven actions for expressing gratitude. Implementing these into your life more frequently can generate both a real-time, almost immediate positive effect on your happiness and health as well as a longer-term, more sustainable improvement in your overall feelings of well-being.

Be Thankful

Take time to be thankful—never taking anyone or anything for granted. Always say thank you—even for little things and even if no one else is there to hear you. Being grateful means having a sense of appreciation, thankfulness, and even wonder

for another person's actions or excellence of moral character that has benefited you, no matter how large or small the
impact. And being grateful encourages moral behavior—the
more you appreciate how fortunate you are and how others
may have helped you, the more inclined you are to reciprocate
with thoughtful, kind, and caring actions yourself.

Count Your Blessings

Concentrate for a few moments on the things you are grateful
for—literally "count your blessings." Make a mental list of
the good things about yourself and about your life and even
about life on this planet in general. Resist the lure of negative
thoughts—complaining only breeds unhappiness. Force yourself to focus on the things that are good in your life. Taking a
moment to emphasize and appreciate what's good about your
life right now tempers negative feelings of envy and mutes
some of your anxiety about the past, present, and future—and
less anxiety equals more happiness. Counting your blessings
even for just a few moments is an important counterbalance
to the ills and spills of everyday life.

Daily Gratitude Inventory

Take what is called a gratitude inventory. Daily, write down a list
of everything about yourself and everything you have for which
you are grateful—instead of being envious about what others
have that you want. Don't limit your list to only those fortunate
happenings that affect you directly—be grateful for our world
even with all its faults and for the wonders of everyday nature
around you—appreciating these can be a balm for your soul.
Reread your gratitude inventory list whenever you wish to help
keep your perspective amid the tests and trials of life.

Weekly Gratitude Journal

Spend fifteen minutes once every week—preferably on Sunday evening—and record your blessings from the past week in a gratitude journal that you keep for just that purpose.

The process could work something like this:

- First, consider all aspects of your life, large and small, that you might be grateful for including both events that happened and people who have had a positive impact on your life during the past week.

- Then, use Kipling's "six honest serving men" to help guide your thinking—recalling *what* you are grateful for, *why* you feel that way, *where* positive experiences have happened, *who* has influenced your life, and *when* and *how* has it been enriched.

- After contemplating your life in the past week using this process, write down five things for which you are grateful in your gratitude journal.

Do this on a regular weekly basis. Vary the timing and frequency if needed. Even writing in a journal for as few as three weeks can create a meaningful difference in your level of happiness.

Gratitude Buddy

Find a gratitude partner—called a gratitude buddy—with whom you can share your gratitude journal. Sharing your gratitude with a buddy—either a family member or a close friend—has the power and potential to enrich your gratitude experience and enhance your appreciation of all that is good in your life.

Gratitude Letter

Write a gratitude letter to a specific person who has exerted a positive influence on your life—but whom you've never personally thanked. If a loved one, consider including a list of ten positive things about the person you are writing to. If appropriate for you, consider including some form of art to visually express your feelings.

Once your gratitude letter is written, seriously consider directly expressing your gratitude by actually mailing your letter or making a phone call and reading your letter aloud. Even though these last steps may be particularly poignant, however, they are not required. Just writing the letter is sufficient to increase your feelings of happiness.

Gratitude Visit

Even better, though, is—after writing your gratitude letter—to call the person in advance to schedule a "gratitude visit." But don't mention the purpose of the visit on the call. Then, when you arrive, read your gratitude letter aloud and give the person a copy. One example might be to write and then visit and read your letter to a favorite teacher from your school days who positively impacted your life.

Remember: although mailing your gratitude letter or holding a gratitude visit can be particularly meaningful for both parties, simply writing the gratitude letter and not delivering it can produce substantial boosts in happiness. It is the awakening of your feelings of thankfulness that yields the benefits.

Gratitude Tour

Look for opportunities to introduce a visitor to the people, places, and things that you love—often giving you a fresh perspective and increased appreciation for your life and the people in it.

Keys to Success

Select some or all of these proven strategies for expressing gratitude and add them to your daily and weekly life. But don't over-practice them, or they will lose their power and become routine. For optimal benefit, don't hesitate to vary the timing, frequency, or other details of how, when, and how often you pause and reflect and express your gratitude. The goal is to train yourself to perform these proven actions more frequently as a normal part of your life.

A CHOICE

For a happier life, choose to live your life with a grateful attitude. Expressing thankfulness for and even relishing positive life experiences and circumstances gives you the gift of deriving the maximum satisfaction and enjoyment from your life no matter what it may have been or may be today. But if the idea of expressing gratitude makes you feel uncomfortable or if you don't want to write or talk about your feelings or if you don't want to feel obligated to a person who has helped you, of course the choice is yours. Only you can weigh the sustained, long-term benefits of heightened happiness against your hesitancy and discomfort with the process. Done sincerely, expressing gratitude can transform your life.

PERFORM ACTS OF KINDNESS

Be kind, for everyone you meet is fighting a hard battle.

— Plato, Greek philosopher (427–347 B.C.)

Increase the frequency with which you perform acts of kindness—both for your loved ones and for others. Create and implement a conscious and intentional kindness strategy—it is a proven path to maximizing the amount of happiness you receive. Ironically, being kind to others is in your own self-interest. Your kindness helps them while at the same time makes you feel uplifted—elevated even—and, thus, happier. You, for at least one moment, personify all that is good about humankind. And these feelings of self-gratification can last for a whole day and longer.

Commit to perform five acts of kindness each week—all in one day if possible. They don't need to be grandiose or complicated, nor all for one person, and they can range from small, simple acts to grand gestures. The options are unlimited when it comes to acts of kindness. But choose carefully. Plan your day and vary the acts of kindness so they stay meaningful and don't just become a chore. Be consciously kinder to spouse, family, friends and acquaintances, classmates and coworkers—but also to strangers. Everyone has their struggles.

Even in the busiest of times, always take time to do a favor—a good and kind deed for others—even if they aren't close friends. Try to perform these acts of kindness as often as you can—there are so many people less fortunate than you. Resolve to include one kind act every week about which you tell no one—your feelings of intrinsic worth will be deepened by the absence of external reinforcement.

Be as excited about others' good fortune as you are about

your own. If needed and possible, take responsibility for someone's well-being—even if only temporarily. Donate time or money or both if you can. Write to a grandparent. Each day, try to tell someone something you like, appreciate, or admire about them. Be empathetic about the trials and suffering of others—they didn't ask for and most likely didn't do anything to deserve what has become their lot in life. Always remember what we all know deep inside: how easily and quickly—in a heartbeat—you could share their fate. Offer a shoulder of sympathy in times of distress and pain; sometimes the burden of life is almost too heavy for one person to bear alone.

The value of kindness is not a new concept. For centuries, philosophers, religious leaders, teachers, parents, and writers too many to count have extolled its goodness. For some of us, kindness comes naturally—our inner character is a kind one. For others, a conscious and intentional effort is needed. But, no matter how you are wired, it is possible to perform kind acts for others and bask in the special feelings these acts engender within you—even if the kindness is difficult or unpleasant and you receive nothing in return. And, as long as your acts of kindness are voluntary, spontaneous, sensitive to others' wishes, and pose no risk to your own well-being, exercising your character and rising to the occasion of helping another has many benefits. It can not only positively affect your self-perception by giving you reason to view yourself as a kind and compassionate soul, it can give you a renewed appreciation of your own good fortune. And your acts of kindness may also inspire others to perform kindnesses—creating a ripple effect of goodness.

The power and magic lie in consciously increasing the number of days you spend performing acts of kindness for others. This increases your level of happiness—and often for an extended period of time. If you are sincere and dedicated in implementing your kindness strategy, you may even uncover a secret that some of the wealthiest have already discovered: people are often happier spending their time and money on others rather than on themselves.

Many of the most important things in life share this other-focused secret.

BE MORE EXTROVERTED

Acting extroverted makes people happier.

—William Fleeson, Associate Professor of Psychology, Wake Forest University

Strive to intentionally become more extroverted—to more frequently act outgoing and be more sociable—even if your natural tendency is to be introverted. The theory of introverts living happier lives because they are more isolated and insulated from the world and therefore less stressed has turned out in repeated studies to be a myth. Instead, anxiety and depression are more common among introverts than extroverts. It is extroverts who are the happier ones—their day-to-day experiences are pleasanter and more joy-filled. They are more cheerful and high-spirited and more self-assured. They can more easily walk into a room full of strangers and introduce themselves—maybe because they are more accepting of themselves and are more confident others will like them. And they are more likely to have gotten married, found good jobs, made new close friends. Not a bad report card.

So, make people a priority. Approach others more directly. Make eye contact. Develop a more outgoing social personality by asking more questions, voicing your opinions, listening more actively, and showing more verbal and nonverbal signs of agreement while others are talking with you.

Restructure your life to spend more time socializing to build a broader network of friends. As we have seen, there is evidence that happiness is contagious, so you may actually feel happier just by witnessing more joy because you are out socially more often and are more apt to be involved in groups and celebrations. Remember, you don't need to befriend everyone in town—in fact, your well-being depends more on the strength and depth of individual relationships than on their number. Just reach out more to others—extroversion is about your interpersonal behavior, not your living arrangements or occupation or work environment. Extroverts are happier whether they live and work alone or with others.

Although personality traits like extroversion do have moderate genetic predispositions, there is room for nurture's influence as well. Even introverts can become happier by acting in more extroverted ways—with one caution. For *some* introverts, acting in a way that is counter to their personality and use of their quiet strengths—like solitude, reflection, and quiet exploration of ideas—can be stressful and depleting.

Still, with this caution in mind, like the other strategies in this imperative, since actions lead attitudes, begin to act more outgoing and soon you will be.

PRACTICE FORGIVENESS

To err is human, to forgive, divine.
—Alexander Pope, English poet (1688–1744)

Be more forgiving of imperfections and mistakes—those of others and especially of your own. Never forget that we are all imperfect human beings, subject in varying degrees to our instinctual primitive nature. Ironically, it is this very imperfection that makes forgiveness relevant. Try to give all people—even strangers—a second chance whenever possible. Work to overcome your natural human tendency to seek revenge—to try to get even when attacked, hurt, wronged, or offended by another person or persons. Instead, let one of your guiding values be forgiveness.

Be clear: forgiving others for their wrongs is something you do to benefit *yourself,* not those who have wronged you. Without surrendering your core beliefs, decide to practice forgiveness in as many situations as you can in response to slights, hurts, violations, and betrayals. Choose to forgive in order to move on with your life instead of staying mired in persistent ruminations about reciprocating with equal harm, avoiding the person forever, or seeking revenge. Long extolled and advocated by both psychological and religious traditions, forgiveness reduces your pain, hostility, helplessness, resentment, and anger toward the perpetrator—all of which damage you emotionally and even physically and often prevent you from living a happier life. Deny the transgressor that much power over your thoughts and feelings.

But what about forgiving you? Forgiving yourself for your errant ways can prevent you from staying stuck in a cycle of negativity and self-blame. Mistakes you make can be invaluable lessons. And forgiveness is the antidote to perfectionism. The negative feelings you feel from blaming yourself are often doubly difficult to avoid since they are directed *at* you *by* you. And, if taken to extremes, such negativity may bar you from a happier life. Choosing to forgive yourself by saying "Welcome to the human race" when you inevitably err allows you to move on with your life.

To Forgive or Not to Forgive

Forgive those who have wronged you when you can—but consider: for some, it may be desirable to forgive but not necessarily restore closeness with the transgressor. For others, you may both forgive and reestablish a close relationship—and for still others, you may find their transgressions to be inexcusable and unforgivable. The choice is yours.

Whichever choice you make, your decision to practice forgiveness is not some immutable mandate for all situations for the remainder of your life. Forgiveness is situational—and the decision is always yours to make in each individual case. It is up to each of us to weigh the pros and cons of forgiveness and decide how forgiving a person do we want to be. Try to strike a balance. While forgiving may diminish your desire to get even, it can also feel like a lack of empathy for the victim, in this case: yourself. Still, the act of forgiving can free you from the grip of your negative emotions and transform your anger, bitterness, and hate into understanding and even empathy for the transgressor. Done sincerely, forgiveness can even restore your physical health, improve your relationships, and give you greater feelings of hope, compassion, and peace—making you more likely to be more agreeable, more serene, and, yes, happier.

The Process of Forgiveness

True forgiveness is not "forgive and forget," not reconciliation with the person who injured you, and not excusing, condoning, justifying, minimizing, or tolerating the offense. Instead, true forgiveness means making the often-difficult effort to shift your thinking to better understand and try to empathize with the perpetrator's thoughts, motives, and emotions—and, as a result, maybe feel sympathy and even compassion for that person. The better you can see things from someone else's perspective and empathize with them, the more likely you are to eventually be able to forgive them. Why did they do what they did? Was it deliberate? Were there extenuating circumstances? Could it have been you instead of them? As an example, if seriously hurt by a drunk driver, consider if you've ever driven when you shouldn't have. Maybe they—and you if you were injured—were just unlucky.

To forgive, recall the hurt or violation and try to empathize. Commit to rise above your desire for revenge and to forgive instead. Write the apology letter you would have liked to receive from the transgressor—apologies humanize people and produce empathy. Then write your letter of forgiveness—pouring all your feelings of anger, bitterness, and blame into this letter, describing how you were and maybe still are hurt and state what you wish the other person had done instead—ending with your statement of forgiveness. But don't send the letter. Whether you choose to take this one final step and make contact with the perpetrator to communicate your forgiveness is situational and up to you to decide. It is not required for true forgiveness. You may choose to just treat the transgressor as you treat everyone else in your life.

Remember: true forgiveness is for your benefit and yours alone—your purpose is to regain power over your feelings and emotions. It is the act of forgiveness on your part that grants you freedom from your negative thoughts and painful emotions and that leads to increased happiness.

And this act of forgiveness is something you can do yourself.

Your choice to forgive helps change and heal your hurt feelings. Remember that your pain and suffering are coming from your memory of and feelings about an event that occurred sometime in the past, and not directly from the event itself. With that in mind, you may feel freer to transform your feelings even though you can't change your memory (or the reality) of the past event itself. Like it or not, the past is immutable.

WHERE TO GO FROM HERE

First, determine if there are people still in your life or situations from your past that you have never forgiven—and whether your lack of forgiveness and persistent dwelling on past circumstances is still causing you pain or not. If so, consider practicing forgiveness with regard to them, beginning now. Your present happiness may be being held prisoner by your pain from past wrongs.

Second, beyond healing any past hurts, make practicing forgiveness a habit from now on—whenever new or past resentments or ruminations arise. Your decision to forgive can prevent these ills from intruding on the happier life you are seeking. Decide whether to forgive or not at least in part by assessing which choice might yield the greater happiness for you. Remember that the best revenge for most violations is still a life well lived.

Although practicing forgiveness is one of the more difficult happiness-increasing actions, stay motivated to succeed. In a larger sense, true forgiveness can deepen your connection to your own humanity—a comforting reminder that you are not alone in dealing with the imperfections of others and of yourself, and with the inevitable slings and arrows that are a part of a full life.

FIND MORE FLOW

> *In the writing of [Tolstoy's] books, there had to be such ecstasy as few men ever know—the pleasure of artistic genius in full command of its powers. As in Mozart's composition, Socrates' philosophizing, Michelangelo's painting and sculpture and poetry and architecture, there is a potency that makes it possible to speak of a man as being godlike.*
>
> —Martine de Courcel, Tolstoy biographer

Find ways to be "in the flow" (or "in the zone")—a state of total engagement—more frequently in as many situations as possible in your personal and professional life. Flow yields an immediate pleasurable high and a feeling of productiveness while you are in a flow state, and you emerge from such a state with a longer-lasting feeling of enjoyment that increases your self-esteem and sense of competence.

What Is Flow?

Most people have experienced being "in the flow" at one time or another—even if they have never heard the term. Popularized by the father of flow, Mihaly Csikszentmihalyi, *flow* is a state of intense, complete absorption and involvement—a total engagement in what you're doing in the moment. You are fully concentrating, completely focused only on the activity and unaware of yourself. Nothing distracts you. You have a deep but effortless involvement that is totally absorbing. You lose yourself in the activity—and you lose track of time. Self-consciousness disappears. You don't worry about failure. It is as if you are riding a wave where you just know what to do and you do it—totally relaxed, certain you are right. Flow activities—usually a combination of physical and mental processes—are challenging, engrossing, and difficult enough to stretch your skills and expertise to their limits—but without overwhelming you. Properly balancing the level of challenge against the level of skill required is the key. If challenges overwhelm your skills, anxiety and frustration will follow. But if challenges are too easy, boredom results. For many, the intrinsic rewards from being "in the flow" mean more than any external rewards or money or prestige they may receive from the results of the work.

While few can claim to be the equal of Tolstoy or Mozart or Socrates or Michelangelo, for everyone, almost any mentally or physically active pursuit can give a feeling of being "in the zone." Examples abound: athletes, chess players, dancers, artists, performers, writers, programmers, knitters and quilters, woodworkers, surgeons, sailors, mountain climbers. Some of the happiest moments can occur when "in the flow" in active pursuits such as these.

Finding Flow

Seek to increase the frequency of flow experiences in all areas of your life—school, work, hobbies and interests, passions, volunteering. You can also find them in the mundane tasks that are a part of daily life for us all.

Work. Strive to find work you enjoy that is meaningful and in which you can find flow. Re-craft your job—with help from your employer—into a more meaningful experience during which you can be in a flow state more often. Set your own goals within your job to challenge yourself. Look for opportunities to be creative. Find the flow inherent in meaningful work. Ironically, the "work paradox" says that people tend to seek idleness and prefer leisure to working, yet they find many of their peak flow experiences at work. Idleness and escapism may sound like bliss—but the cost is lost opportunities for flow and joy.

Play. Reassess your use of leisure time. While some downtime is necessary to combat life's chaos, the amount of pure leisure needed varies during the various stages of life. Try to reduce the time spent in inactive pursuits like TV watching, listening to music, and vegging out to the minimum needed for rest. Passive activities such as these, while enjoyable, are never fully engaging. And, if done in excess, they can lead to self-absorption, a symptom of mild depression.

Bypass these dead-end roads and you will lead a happier life. That is, strive to turn passive leisure boredom into active mental and physical activities that bring their own flow—and enjoyment. Choose activities where you can fully engage your skills without being overwhelmed, then set goals and immerse yourself so you are in the zone—and can emerge exhilarated and triumphant.

Daily life. Look for opportunities to create something new—either at work or at home. Creative processes engage you totally in flow and allow you to feel transcendent in the use of your skills and powers. When you find these creative opportunities, craft a strategy to spend more time immersed in them—without ignoring your responsibilities for yourself and for the others in your life.

Learn until the day you die. Be open to learning new things as often as possible—and approach them with the rapt attention and concentration of a young child learning new things every second. To perpetuate enjoyment, continually increase complexity. Develop a habit of concentrating fiercely on any and every thing you do—even the most routine of tasks—approaching them as if you are creating a masterpiece. This approach will allow you to transform time spent doing routine tasks into "microflow" opportunities. Similarly, create stimulating mind games to challenge yourself when engaged in any of life's tedious yet essential activities—vacuuming, driving in bumper-to-bumper traffic, waiting for appointments or public transportation, cleaning. Solve puzzles in your mind. Think of new, alternate lyrics to your favorite songs. Add flow to conversations by actively listening—focus your attention so intently you don't notice the sights and sounds around you.

Train yourself to find opportunities to achieve a state of flow—total engagement—in as many situations as possible. You can sometimes feel increased feelings of happiness both *before* and *after* you engage in an activity due to its importance, but equally happy feelings can be yours *during* almost any activity if you are in the flow.

EMBRACE FITNESS AND HEALTH

> Mens sana in corpore sano *(a sound mind in a sound body)*
>
> —Famous Latin maxim

Revel in the wonder that is good health for as long as your life permits—health is the precious yet instantly changeable foundation upon which all happiness is built. Guard it well. Fight the good fight to minimize risks of the two major causes of serious illness and death—heart disease and cancer—while graciously surrendering to the natural decline in health that comes with age. Adopt a healthy lifestyle and adjust your diet and habits—smoking, drinking, eating, and drugs. They affect your health and your mood. Although people adapt quite well to ill health, serious illnesses—especially chronic, disabling ones—can significantly erode happiness. Yet good health is only barely related to the level of happiness someone feels. People are upset more by ill health than they are made happy by good health. In this way, health resembles wealth: its absence can breed misery but its presence is no guarantee of happiness.

Embrace the fitness movement—it is a reliable road to a happier life in the long term as well as a short-term instant happiness boost. If your health permits, immediately incorporate some form of exercise into your daily routine—walking, jogging, running, dancing, playing a sport. Any fitness regimen—and preferably one that includes aerobic exercise—will pay benefits. And these benefits are not just physical: seeing yourself accomplish something raises your self-esteem and gives you a respite from day-to-day stress, and it makes you more self-confident and resilient. You can even live longer. Regular exercise—20 to 30 minutes per day for four or five days a week—improves heart and lung fitness and lessens stress and mild depression. In some cases, exercise can even work better than anti-depression medications—with less chance of relapse. If you can, exercise strenuously—the benefits can last for hours. For healthy women, moderate physical activity such as just walking briskly for one hour a day can maintain your weight during your middle years. And become more consciously aware of your carriage: stand straighter and more upright without slouching. Remember, any energy use above a resting level has benefits, so options are unlimited. Do something you enjoy—and reap the benefits. Don't overdo. Virtually anyone at any age can benefit from just moving around more each day. Seek support if you need it—expertise and professional assistance to increase health and fitness are on virtually every corner.

Move more, beginning today. Scientific study has now confirmed what you've probably been hearing for most of your life: regular physical activity is good for you—it is not only a reliable route to make you healthier and fitter, it will also make you happier. Not unexpectedly, a predictable virtuous cycle is at work: embracing fitness and good health makes you feel happier and feeling happy and fulfilled also contributes to your good health.

PRACTICE MEDITATION

All of humanity's problems stem from man's inability to sit quietly in a room alone.

—Blaise Pascal, French mathematician and philosopher
(1623–1662)

Make the regular practice of meditation a ritual in your daily life. No matter which meditation technique you choose, it is the regular practice of it that will benefit your level of happiness and even your physical well-being. Consider the many types of meditation techniques that are available, choose one, study and learn it and begin your practice. It can be as simple as just being mindful of the present moment without distractions. Detaching yourself from your daily stresses—even if only for a short period of time each day—always yields benefits.

Although the successful practice of meditation may be performed in a myriad of different ways—the details of which are a personal choice—one key step is to set a regular schedule for your meditation for 10 to 60 minutes, preferably at the same time each day. No matter whether it is first thing in the morning or at lunch or in the evening, block out this time on your calendar and guard it zealously against any changes. With practice, you can even enjoy benefits in as few as one or two minutes—allowing you to meditate whenever you feel stressed or upset or whenever you want some stillness amid the bustle of everyday life. Meditation mastery allows you to achieve a peaceful moment wherever you are whenever you need one.

While meditation has many rewards, it is not a quick fix. Like all of the proven strategies, it is a discipline that requires regular, daily focused practice for an extended period of time. Whether you choose to meditate to reduce anxiety and stress, improve your mood, gain a momentary respite of inner peace, attain insight, or inspire creativity, you can also improve your physical health and realize increased happiness in the process.

STAY RESTED

To do great work, a man must be very idle as well as very industrious.

— Samuel Butler, English novelist (1835–1902)

Adopt a gentle discipline to reserve enough time to stay rested. Sufficient sleep is a basic ingredient that allows you to awaken each morning refreshed and revitalized—ready to begin an active day in a positive mood to live a full, active, industrious, and happy life.

Listen to your body. Strive to get seven or eight hours of sleep a night. Nap during days as needed. Even one additional hour of sleep each night can help you fight the effects of the sleep deprivation epidemic that is engulfing modern society: fatigue, a run-down feeling, less alertness, moods of gloom and even mild depression. Not exactly a recipe for health or happiness.

Staying rested is not easy—we all suffer from occasional sleeplessness, and wakeful alertness is a natural response when facing threats or feeling stressed. And with increasing age, uninterrupted sleep often recedes into a sweet memory from younger times.

Even though sometimes challenging to achieve, renewing rest will give you a solid foundation of energy to triumph over life's daily perils. It is an essential if you are to make a meaningful contribution to the world—and to achieve a healthy and happier life as a result.

SEEK RENEWING SOLITUDE

It is in silence, and not in commotion, in solitude and not in crowds, that God best likes to reveal himself.
—Thomas Merton, American Catholic writer (1915–1968)

Seek renewing solitude—often it is only in stillness and tranquility that life's truths reveal themselves. Have you experienced this phenomenon? Sometimes major insights and truths arrive unbidden in the quiet moment—insights that are too often drowned out by the unrelenting noise of everyday life.

Balance the busyness of life by allocating sufficient time to spend with yourself. Even small doses of renewing solitude—a few minutes daily of private, quiet time for meditation or prayer or just enjoying a moment of stillness with you and yourself alone—can provide the necessary recharging for a happier, more productive, and longer life. Set aside one or two times each day for "quiet time"—solitary time with no distractions—when you are not working, doing errands, or playing the various roles of your life (parent, spouse, worker, boss, sibling, child) and enjoy contemplative silence without commotion. Rest your brain—and do so several times per day. Bask in the stillness. When you can, lie on your back and count clouds or stars—meditative relaxation is an antidote to stress and can result in a greater sense of tranquility and inward stillness as well as lowered blood pressure and heightened immune system defenses.

Beyond this quiet self-discipline, consider a day of soul-searching solitude via a technique called R.E.S.T. (Restricted Environmental Stimulation Therapy)—lying quietly alone on a comfortable bed in the monotonous, isolated environment of a darkened, soundproofed room with sufficient food, water, and comforts—and without interruption. R.E.S.T. is a pleasant and stress-free way of reducing external stimulation. And the healing power of the quiet solitude can yield inspiration—deep insights into yourself, your personality, your life—and a new feeling of oneness with the universe. Experiments by University of British Columbia researcher Peter Suedfeld found that a day of R.E.S.T. has helped people increase their self-control—allowing them to gain or lose weight, drink less, speak more fluently, reduce hypertension and stress, overcome irrational fears, boost self-confidence, and stop smoking.

Solitude has been known to work wonders for creativity, too. Philosophers, scientists, artists, religious leaders, and visionaries have all benefited from being freed from distractions—often triggering vivid fantasies, ideas, and deep inspirations and insights that would perhaps have remained unreachable amid the daily cacophony of sound and intrusions. In cultures around the world—among Japanese, Africans, Australians, and Native Americans—solitude is a proven route to maturity, spiritual recharging, and improved self-belief. Even people who have been shipwrecked or placed in solitary confinement or on a solitary voyage have reported that while it can be traumatic—some feel threatened, helpless, or malnourished—others find a positive side in feelings of a deep spiritual experience, a new relationship with God, a feeling of oneness with the ocean or the universe, or a life-changing new insight into their personalities.

There is a season for all levels of activity. The renewing power of a day of R.E.S.T. reduces the external noise and stimulation and allows you to hear your own small internal voices. In today's 24/7 world, it is ironic that the healing powers of renewing solitude are, more than ever, being reaffirmed. It turns out that one part of the process of living a happier life includes being both very active and very idle.

EMBRACE SPIRITUALITY

> *We are not human beings on a spiritual journey. We are spiritual beings on a human journey.*
> —Stephen Covey, author of *The 7 Habits of Highly Effective People*

Seek to embrace spirituality. Select either a religious or a secular search for meaning in life that is signaled by believing in something larger than yourself. People can be spiritual because they have a set of moral values or because they feel elevated in a beautiful setting—without necessarily believing in a deity or worshipping with others in a religious group.

Whether you choose to join and actively participate in an organized religion of your choice, to adopt and practice your own private religious faith, or to add a sense of spirituality to your secular system of beliefs, more fully embracing spirituality can increase your happiness, improve your life, and help your health. Recall that moving beyond a self-focused life is critical for well-being—and spirituality helps answer the most fundamental need humans have: to know that we matter and that our lives matter and have some significance, meaning, and purpose. Actually having faith in something beyond yourself gives you this meaning.

For billions of people the world over, having faith and a belief in some form of religion or spirituality increases the sense of hope, gratitude, love, awe, compassion, and joy—all of which increase happiness. Having a sense of spirituality also helps you avoid delinquency, physical illnesses, drug and alcohol abuse, divorce, and suicide while providing an improved ability to cope with the inevitable stress, crises, and losses that life brings to everyone.

You can receive spiritual support by having faith in your supportive relationship with a God that lets you feel unconditionally loved, accepted as you are and cared for. And belonging to a community of like-minded people also provides you with higher levels of social support. Many, particularly the older among you, take great comfort that, no matter what happens, it's all according to "God's plan" and every happening—even the unthinkable—has some meaning and purpose, even if they aren't privy to what it is. They trust that their God will show them the way and help guide them through their lives—giving them a feeling of security, peace, and calm. In times of trial, what is called "religious coping"—the belief that whatever happened is God's will—is the most frequently used form of coping to help people adjust by providing hope in the chaos and darkness that events are not random but have a meaning and a purpose and are part of a divine plan. And having a sense of a higher purpose in their lives helps them to ponder the universal query about the meaning of life that comes to everyone in time. What is it all about, Alfie, anyway?

Whatever the specific reasons, there is no question that some form of spirituality increases feelings of well-being. Three approaches can help you embrace spirituality more fully in your life:

- Join and practice a religion of your choosing.
- Keep the faith.
- Adopt secular spirituality.

Join and Practice a Religion of your Choosing

Become more religiously active and incorporate religion into your daily life—actively religious people are happier. Attend church services more frequently. Spend more time in social situations with clergy and fellow members of the congregation. Pray more often, either alone or with groups at specific times depending on your religion of choice. Read scripture alone or in a study group. Sanctify day-to-day experiences by making them sacred. Join your religious community in performing acts of charity or meditation. Bask in the comfort of knowing that your God is watching out for you—much as your parents hopefully watched out for you in your youth. Organized religion can simplify life by providing a unifying set of values, rules, rituals, and guidelines to follow that help deal with the sometimes overwhelming options and complexities of life today.

Comfort is sometimes derived more from having conviction and trust in a set of religious beliefs than from their specific content. Implement the tools and tenets of your chosen religion frequently at all stages of life—from the early years through the teens into adulthood. All groups of all ages can increase their happiness by practicing religion more actively—and regain lost happiness more rapidly after a crisis. Faith-based religious organizations have been found to be quite effective in providing social and community services including education, financial support, housing, clothing, food, and psychological counseling to those in need.

Keep the Faith

Choose to practice your religious faith privately by following the practices of your religion on your own—outside of the formal organization. Cultivate your own closer relationship with your chosen God in your own way. Set aside between five and sixty minutes daily for prayer. Recite passages from a prayer book. Ask your God to guide and protect you and grant specific wishes. Recite prayers of gratitude—they can be especially comforting. Develop a prayer or meditation ritual to enhance your inner being. Think quietly to clarify your sense of what life is all about. Simply sit quietly for 15 minutes a day and listen to the silence. Pursue goals that reflect your true self—and the contribution you wish to make to the planet. Transcend yourself by using your creativity to help others and to better mankind. Consider some form of community with like-thinking people. Even if not in an organized religious setting, a spiritually guided group, faith community, or prayer group can serve well. Any faith that offers self-acceptance, a sense of hope, some community and outward focus, and a view of life's meaning can yield valuable perspective during life's inevitable highs and lows.

Adopt Secular Spirituality

Develop and follow your own nonreligious belief system. The benefits of being more spiritual can still be felt by those for whom conventional religious beliefs are difficult or impossible in this scientific, secular age.

Define your own meaningful rituals. Create your own prayer—perhaps focusing on gratitude. Clarify your beliefs about why you are here and the meaning of life—people can find meaning and purpose in life without the influence of faith. Sanctify various important aspects of your life. For example, see your children as blessings, believe in eternal love, treat parenting as a sacred duty, revere your body as a temple and believe that marriage is a sacred bond. By giving areas of your life divine qualities, you can gain feelings of meaning, motivation, and increased satisfaction akin to those that others derive from organized religious activities. Attend retreats to broaden your inner beliefs. Focus on daily walking, jogging, hiking, crafting, knitting, or cooking routines to free your mind from distractions and create quiet space, and you will gain some peace similar to that from prayer or meditation.

Dare to be alone with yourself and your thoughts in silence. If appropriate, embrace a reasoned, scientific approach to explain your human origins. If you doubt that God created the universe, try a belief in intelligent design by a benevolent overseer—this view can provide comfort. Choose to join a group of like-thinking people—the feelings of community, love, and support that religion provides can be available to nonbelievers too.

Caution. Sadly but not surprisingly, some cautions about spirituality are in order. Be careful in the type of God you choose to believe in—some belief systems are filled with bigotry, prejudice, and even hate and violence against nonbelievers. Use moderation and common sense in your spiritual practices. Beware of strict conformity to strict expectations for family life and morality and be wary of excessive demands on your time, energy, and money. Acknowledge that there are limitations to the power of faith. Blind adherence to dogma such as "prayer alone can cure illnesses" can lead to irresponsible health decisions. Even the strongest of faiths will not guarantee a loss-free life. Disillusionment is the certain destiny of those who believe otherwise. And finally, resist passively deferring all problems to your God—this is an indicator of lower levels of mental health.

WELCOME THE SPIRITUAL

Within limits, find and embrace an articulate spirituality—whether religious or secular—and add religious tools such as prayer and reading of spiritual writings to your daily life. Whatever form of faith you choose, remember that faith is just that—a leap of faith—a bet that belief in the absence of evidence can help you shape your future and your hopes and dreams in an uncertain world. Let these beliefs guide your actions and help you live a meaningful life—but without deterring your ability to act on your own behalf when needed. Develop a coherent belief system about your purpose on the planet and the meaning of life. You will be happier for your efforts. Finding meaning lets you believe that your work and pain and suffering are not in vain, that you have some control over your life, that your life has a purpose and your contribution to the planet matters. Cultivating a spiritual belief in something larger than yourself allows you to believe you matter—that you are more than just dust in the wind.

TRANSITION

The Third Imperative: Intentionally Act *Happy continues to shift the focus more toward positively affecting others instead of just self-centeredly pleasing yourself. As you will recall, this move from self-focus to other-focused is one key for enduring happiness. The proven actions of this imperative—expressing gratitude, performing acts of kindness, being more extroverted, practicing forgiveness, finding flow, embracing fitness and health, practicing meditation, staying rested, seeking renewing solitude, and embracing spirituality—do more than begin to positively affect those around you. As you implement them into your daily life on a more frequent basis, you also feel frequent positive bursts of happiness lasting for the medium term: days, weeks, and months, and sometimes even longer.*

Although the actions described in The Second Imperative: Intentionally Think *Happy and The Third Imperative: Intentionally* Act *Happy do require somewhat more effort than the pleasure-seeking activities of The First Imperative: Seek Pleasure within Limits, they generate correspondingly greater rewards by tending to create longer-lasting feelings of happiness and by being less subject to adaptation. In short, they are more durable, sustainable, and renewable. Their impact lasts longer than that of simple pleasure seeking, they can be easily repeated, and they increase happiness every time they are integrated into day-to-day life.*

The final three imperatives—The Fourth Imperative: Become a Better Person, The Fifth Imperative: Embrace Loving Connections, and The Sixth Imperative: Make a Meaningful Contribution—are the longest-lasting and most powerful of all. They offer opportunities for fundamental, personal changes and growth—changes that can fill you with the belief and confidence that you can live a life that will make a meaningful difference in the world and will not be in vain.

The feelings of happiness from these last three imperatives can last a lifetime.

CHAPTER 9

THE FOURTH IMPERATIVE: BECOME A BETTER PERSON

> *The most important human endeavor is the striving for morality in our actions. Our inner balance and even our very existence depend on it. Only morality in our actions can give beauty and dignity to life.*
>
> —Albert Einstein, Nobel Prize–winning physicist
> (1879–1955)

Constantly strive to become a better person—to become a good person of good moral character at all moments and in all situations—and to put your unique skills and abilities to their best use. Being both *goods*—a good person of good character—provides a lifelong way to be a better person—and to feel happier just because of who you are.

By *enhancing* the frequency with which you display the positive traits of good character you already have, *embracing* the ones that are new for you, and *maximizing* your skills and abilities, you can behave in ways that can be a powerful, proven source of positive emotions for the remainder of your life.

The Fourth Imperative: Become a Better Person focuses on improving who you are, not just changing how you think and act. When you choose to will yourself to use certain personality traits, skills, and abilities that produce positive and virtuous results—that is, to do the right thing more often—you feel elevated and inspired with feelings of pride, satisfaction, joy, and fulfillment. You are honest when tempted to lie. You are fair and just in all situations. You courageously face your challenges instead of shying away when the going gets tough. You take maximum advantage of your skills and abilities. You persevere in the face of life's inevitable intrusions. And whether or not anyone notices when you act in these ways, *you* feel good, uplifted, even ennobled by your choices.

Furthermore, when you choose to consistently and intentionally live your life in this way—to act as a better person by living according to certain values and maximizing your abilities—in addition to being happier, over time, you *become* that better person. The better the person you become, the happier you feel—and these feelings can last for a lifetime.

So, what are the positive personality traits of a good person of good character?

Many people feel that determining positive traits, morality, values, and virtue are the responsibility of the church. Yet historically, opinions about virtue and morality spring from a huge variety of sources—ancient philosophers in Greece and Rome, thought leaders in virtually all cultures, civilizations, and religions, current-day studies by positive psychologists. In fact, a *moralist* is a person who lives a virtuous or morally excellent life—often without reliance on religion.

The positive traits of good character and those of a good

person that are presented here have been gratefully adapted from Martin Seligman's seminal 2002 book, *Authentic Happiness*, which includes an analysis of more than 200 virtue catalogs spanning 3,000 years, and from Christopher Peterson's 2006 textbook, *A Primer in Positive Psychology*. Each of these traits is ubiquitous around the planet, has inherent value, is typically taught by schools, clubs, and churches, and is what parents in all corners of the world would wish for their newborn children. Most people feel inspired and ennobled when exhibiting these traits and when observing them being practiced by others.

Choosing to increase the frequency with which you exhibit these traits—striving to be a good person of good character—can make you a better person and bring you a happier life, as can maximizing your skills and abilities.

GOOD CHARACTER

Character is Fate.

—André Malraux, French novelist,
adventurer, and statesman (1901–1976)

Strive to become a person of good character. Character consists of the individual, distinctive personality traits that guide a person's observable actions—and can be either good or bad, depending on what mix of virtues and vices have been inherited and developed and shaped by upbringing. Good character is a set of moral traits that conform to generally accepted standards of goodness and rightness. Along with conscience, it is what distinguishes human beings as moral animals, capable of overcoming biologically programmed core tendencies for moral weakness and evil urges including the all-too-frequent penchant for violence towards and killing of fellow humans.

Here are the six families of positive personality traits that, taken together, comprise good character: honesty, courage, wisdom, justice, temperance, and perseverance. The individual traits that make up these six families are italicized for ease of recognition and an enhanced ability to identify the actions needed for implementation. Display these traits more frequently and in new ways, and you will feel inspired and fulfilled by exhibiting your good character. Try to find one new use of a trait each day—doing so can help you more fully realize your potential as a moral human being, and allow you to feel elevated and happier as a result.

Honesty

Strive to be *honest* in word and deed in every situation. Speak your truth quietly but clearly—with sensitivity and tact where required. And always tell the complete truth—lies of omission are just as poisonous as lies of commission. Refrain from telling white lies to family and friends. Minimize insincere compliments. Related family traits:

- *Integrity*. Beyond telling the truth, live your life with *integrity*—it is a real treasure in today's troubled world. Keep your word. It is your one true possession that no one can take from you—and by which you are constantly judged. Stay true to your values and beliefs. And, by doing so, avoid violations of your true self. Keep your promises and follow through on your commitments—doing what you say you will do is the hallmark of personal integrity.

- *Genuineness*. Be yourself. Strive to be a real person—the real you—in all situations. Live your life in a down-to-earth, sincere manner, without pretense. Your *genuineness* allows other people to approach and feel closer to you. Be genuine and honest when explaining your motives to others. By holding true to your core values, you give people around you a chance to also be true to theirs.

Courage

Be courageous—and remember that displaying *valor* in battle is not the only form of *courage*. Stand steadfast for your beliefs even if they are unpopular and may likely bring you negative consequences. Speak out for an unpopular idea in a group if you feel strongly. Protest to the proper authorities if you observe a clear injustice. Related family traits:

- *Bravery*. Perseverance despite fear may be the purest form of *bravery*. As John Wayne, the famous American actor, said: "Courage is being scared to death—but saddling up anyway." Be confident that repetition of a task despite fear will, over time, lessen that fear. Invoke your strong will to strive for goals that are worthy even if you are not certain you can achieve them. Do not shrink from threats, challenges, difficulty, or pain even when fearful. Fear is really only a feeling. Without endangering yourself, fight feeling fearful by deliberately doing something you wouldn't normally do because of your fear.

- *Fortitude*. Face danger squarely—not recklessly or fearlessly but by showing *fortitude* despite your fear even when your physical or mental well-being is threatened. Resist the "flight" behavioral response. Courage allows you to reliably pursue the right ends in fearful situations because you value acting in that way intrinsically. Stay steady in the face of the one aspect of life that is certain: uncertainty. Remain stoic and even cheerful—retaining your sense of dignity—when facing difficult and trying ordeals and serious or even life-threatening illnesses. Be the hero of your own life play—even if there is no audience.

Wisdom and Knowledge

Begin or continue a journey toward *wisdom*—true wisdom is born of *knowledge* tempered with perspective and experience. Be open to new experiences—especially those outside your preconceived notions about the world. Accept and even rejoice in ambiguity—it allows other viewpoints into your life. Related family traits:

- *Curiosity.* Be *curious* and *interested in all aspects of the world* around you and each new thing in your universe. Discover a new place in your town and learn its history. Choose a restaurant with unfamiliar cuisine. Actively engage novelty—the human brain craves the unfamiliar. Fight boredom by trying something new. Seek opportunities to learn, explore, discover, and grow. Be skeptical. Presume nothing. Explore new approaches and gather as much new information as you can in every situation.

- *Love of Learning.* Whether in a formal class or on your own, revel in constantly learning new things. Attend a lecture on a subject about which you know nothing. Read a nonfiction book. Stay open to learning about everything from anyone—friends, family, your elders. Treat all experiences as opportunities to learn. Dare to explore the world around you (but stop short of obsession and sensation seeking). Be thrilled to learn something new each day. Enrich your life by taking a class, reading self-help books, joining a discussion group, or rededicating yourself to your religion. Allocate time and resources to visit museums, to read and to learn anywhere there is opportunity. Learn and use a new word each day.

- *Judgment* and *Critical Thinking*. Optimize your knowledge by using your *judgment* and *critical thinking*. Think challenges through and examine them from all angles. Ask for feedback on your ideas and avoid being defensive—defensiveness prevents growth. Sift through relevant information, thinking rationally and objectively. Don't confuse true facts with your own beliefs. Be willing to challenge pre-existing beliefs. Fight against making snap judgments. Instead of jumping to conclusions, use solid evidence to make decisions—but also value your intuition. Reserve the right to change your mind in the face of new information. Follow the best advice you can find—using your own judgment as to its suitability to your situation.

- *Open-mindedness*. Be *open-minded* about possibilities and willing to consider beliefs and points of view different from your own. Seek new and broader ideas, but also stay respectful of the inviolable truths of the world. Fight against thinking only in ways that confirm what you already believe. Break out of the "one true way" trap. Take a position opposite to your beliefs in a conversation—play the devil's advocate. Truly listen to others' points of view instead of planning what you are going to say in rebuttal. Consider one of your strongest-held positions on a subject—and think about how and why you might be wrong.

- *Ingenuity* and *Originality*. Use your *ingenuity* to reach your goals. Don't content yourself with always doing things the conventional way. Instead, use your *originality* to think of imaginative actions to accomplish your goals. Be flexible: everything changes. And consider creative ways to engage others; most significant goals are not reached alone.

- *Other kinds of intelligence*. Employ your *social intelligence* about the feelings and motives of others in your plans and actions. Be aware of others' moods, temperament, motivations, and intentions, and use this knowledge to inform your decisions and actions. Make someone feel at ease in a social or work situation. Also use your fine-tuned understanding of your own feelings to guide your behavior. If someone annoys or upsets you, try to understand the other person's thought processes and motives instead of retaliating. The set of *social, personal, and emotional intelligence* is fundamental to many traits of personality. Hone your ability to look at situations and the world in ways that make sense to yourself and others.

- *Perspective*. Use your *street smarts* and *perspective* on life's most important challenges to help others solve their problems and develop their own perspective. If asked, offer advice as thoughtfully as you can using your *practical intelligence*. Help resolve disputes among friends, family members, or coworkers by illuminating and illustrating a larger view.

Justice

Be *just* in your decisions that involve other people. Be willing to admit your mistakes and take responsibility for them. Give credit to others if earned, even if you don't especially like them personally. Related family traits:

- *Fairness.* Exhibit *fairness* and act in ways that allow everyone to receive their due. Do not let your personal feelings bias your decisions. Instead, guide your decisions by larger principles of *equity* and fairness. Take the welfare of others as seriously as you do your own. Set aside your personal prejudices and insist that similar situations be treated similarly—fairly and equally—whether you like or even know the people involved or not.

- *Leadership.* When in a *leadership* position, be a humane leader. Be firm in your judgments yet lead with charity for all and without malice. People who are just reliably act that way not merely because they are good at it but also because they place a high intrinsic value on making sure each person receives justice and fairness.

- *Teamwork.* When not in a leadership role, be a loyal and dedicated teammate. Use *teamwork* and work hard for the success of the group. Be a good group *citizen*. Without surrendering your values, respect the group goals and purposes, even when different from your own. Do your *duty*. Never shirk your responsibilities or let your teammates down.

Temperance

Be temperate in satisfying your appetites and desires. Shun gluttony and overindulgence in food, drink, intoxicants, and other pleasures especially including a misplaced desire for the sensuality of food. *Temperance* is the antidote to gluttony. Related family traits:

- *Self-regulation.* Hold your urges in check and wait for appropriate opportunities to satisfy them in *moderation* without harm to yourself or others. Become adept at regulating your emotions—not every feeling you have needs to be acted upon. Fight against your negative feelings so you limit damage to yourself and others. Count to 10 to mute anger. Beyond controlling your feelings, use *discretion* and be careful in your speech and actions. Don't do or say things you might regret later. Refrain from gossiping or saying mean things about others.

- *Prudence.* Avoid high-risk, physically dangerous activities. Think twice before saying anything other than "please" and "thank you." Use your far-sightedness and deliberate manner to make prudent decisions on what course of action is optimal. Make considered choices in friendships and personal relationships.

- *Caution.* Exercise *caution* in today's dangerous world. Resist impulsive thoughts, words, or deeds that could prove short-sighted and jeopardize your achievement of longer-term goals. Act based on what you know to be correct and temperate. It is not enough just to know what's right. Your actions are the truest expressions of your thoughts and beliefs.

- *Modesty.* Believe in yourself—but be *modest* about your accomplishments. Do not unfairly glorify yourself. Shun the spotlight unless called upon. Dress in ways that do not call attention to you. Fight against an excessive love of self out of proportion to your fellow humans. At the same time, avoid insincere, false, or sham modesty—it is a form of boasting. Give respect and credit where they are due. Speak quietly if at all about your aspirations and victories, defeats and suffering—remembering that your story is echoed in everyone's life. Be confident and comfortable in your uniqueness, but avoid trumpeting your own praises in an effort to convince others—and probably mainly yourself—that you're special.

• *Humility.* Be more humble. Fight pretentiousness and consciously work to keep your ego in check. Try to go an entire day without talking about yourself. Instead of bragging about how great you are, let your actions and accomplishments speak for themselves. Receive both praise and criticism with a quiet acceptance—recognizing both triumph and disaster as but brief interludes over the span of a life. Always remember that the Earth is spinning on its axis exactly as it was before you arrived—and will continue long after you depart.

Be recognized and valued for your modesty and humility—they are the antidote and offset to egotism, pride, and vanity—all of which are major barriers to a happier life.

Perseverance: A Catalyst for a Happier Life

In addition to the five classic families of traits of good character, one more trait is absolutely essential: perseverance. That is the one quality that will allow you to more frequently exhibit all the other traits of good character in your life. More significantly, it will also help you live a more meaningful life. In truth, nothing substitutes for perseverance.

Persevere in the face of life's myriad challenges and distractions and temptations. Always finish what you start—including when it comes to becoming a better person. No matter what happens, hang in there. Fight against any tendency to get sidetracked. Take small steps if necessary but keep moving toward your goal. Learn to work for hours at a time without interruptions—and then extend that effort into the days, weeks, months, and even the years it often takes to reach significant goals. Too many people desire instant gratification and give up too soon, before the goal is reached. Anyone who has achieved any success will tell you that perseverance is the key. Overnight success invariably takes longer than one night. Don't stop before the miracle. Be ambitious and dogged in all endeavors—but not at the expense of yourself or others.

CHARACTER DETERMINES DESTINY

Choose to be a person of good character. Maximize your happiness by *enhancing* those good character traits you already have by displaying them more frequently—and by *embracing* other character traits that are less familiar to make them a part of what you do on a regular basis in your daily life.

When it comes to character, we are, in a larger part than we sometimes may like to admit, what our parents made us. And, whether we like it or not, we are what they made us no matter whether it is good or bad. But we are not without choice. We have a say in the matter of our character. No matter what our current stage of human development, all character traits can be both learned and unlearned. It is a signal matter of personal responsibility which type of character we exhibit every minute of our lives.

GOOD PERSON

We must be our own before we can be another's.

—Ralph Waldo Emerson, American essayist, philosopher,
and poet (1803–1882)

In your quest to become a better person, remember that displaying good character is necessary but not sufficient. Simply put, it is also necessary to cultivate and express those traits that, throughout history, good people exhibit. These traits are mostly universal, and some are the historically accepted antidotes to the seven deadly sins of the ancients: pride (including vanity and egotism), greed and avarice, lust, anger and wrath, envy (including jealousy and bigotry), sloth (including idleness and wastefulness of time), and gluttony.

There are five additional families of traits necessary for being a good person. These five extend the concept of a good person beyond the individual traits already presented in earlier chapters, such as optimism, resilience, kindness, gratitude, and forgiveness. To become a good person, you also need to embrace and display the following additional traits more frequently in your daily life.

Generosity

Be *generous* with your time, your money, and your attention—not only to friends, family, and acquaintances but even to strangers. Everyone can use a helping hand every now and again. Volunteer your help whenever you see the opportunity. Do something for someone else as often as you can. When you give of yourself, you feel more connected to others—and you feel good about yourself. Reach out to help another who needs comfort. Whether you write a thank-you note, compliment a coworker, fix your spouse's favorite meal, or volunteer your time at a charity, giving of yourself will make you happier.

Temper your excessive love for money and power and your desire to possess more than you need or can use. Greed is a predictable result of any affluent and materialistic, money-centered culture, where the "pursuit of happiness"—a public happiness for the greater civic good—has been diminished to become the pursuit of *my* happiness. Yet, ironically, as presented in Chapter 3, the selfish pursuit of money and material possessions is doomed to fail as a path to lasting happiness because of adaptation. A truer path is to be kind and generous toward others. Even if you don't really feel that way initially, you'll feel better about yourself when you choose the gift of giving. *Generosity* is the antidote to greed and avarice. Giving, not getting, is one of the secrets to living a happier life. But don't underestimate the power and pervasiveness of greed: you needn't look far to notice how the selfishness of the few will often overwhelm the goodness of the many.

Zeal, Industry, and Related Traits

Fill your life with activities and passions so that you wake up each morning looking forward to the day. Fight against moping about your life or about events over which you have no influence or control.

- *Zeal* and *zest*. Let your *passion* and *enthusiasm* be contagious—other people are inspired by and enjoy being caught up in feelings of *zest, zeal*, and fervor. Allow your spirit to shine through—it can sometimes be the only light visible in other people's lives, so share it when you can. Cultivate an enthusiastic devotion to goals, good causes, and ideals in which you believe. Then be both passionate and *diligent* in working hard toward their furtherance. Become a more spirited and energetic person—laziness forces others to work harder and idleness fosters unhappiness. Do things because you want to and not because you have to.

- *Industry.* Within healthy limits, throw yourself into everything you are involved in. Work as hard as is necessary to achieve your goals. Use your *industriousness* to take on difficult challenges—and complete them with few complaints and lots of enjoyment and pleasure. Be flexible and realistic about what you can accomplish—and be *diligent* in your approach and your work. Enthusiasm and hard work are the antidotes to sloth, idleness, laziness, and wastefulness of time. Be a force of nature when pursuing your passions. Don't be afraid to use yourself up in pursuit of your dreams.

Humanity

Love your fellow man—and woman. Acknowledge the worth of other human beings by taking their interests as seriously as you take your own. Be inclusive in your thinking and your actions and remind yourself what you have in common with others instead of focusing on what divides you. Foster empathy and sympathy for others as part of your belief system rather than isolating yourself. Believe that all people have their stories and are valuable members of humanity.

A love of *humanity* is the antidote to hatred—and hatred has no role in the world today—or any other day. Remember that most hatred of others has its roots in self-hate, so be kind to others. Be guided in your actions by their best interests as well as your own. Share your good fortune with others, remembering that on a planet as small as ours, we all share a destiny.

Tolerance and Related Traits

Tolerance is essential in an imperfect world. And so, too, are patience, mercy, chastity, and meekness. As the antidotes to anger, wrath, and lust, they are one barrier to the incivility, disrespect, lawlessness, and violence that threaten civil society.

- *Tolerance.* Be tolerant of others. In particular, be gentle and patient with the young, understanding of the aged, empathetic with those who work, and accepting of those who do not—and equally tolerant of both the weak and the strong. At one moment or another in your life, chances are that you will have been all of these. Rail against discrimination, bigotry, and hatred—they are a blight upon the landscape and should be an affront to your sensibilities.

Whether or not you believe it, we all have a right to be here. Strive to tolerate the diversity that is our planet today—diversity of color, thought, rights, ideas, education, age, and religious beliefs. The conundrum remains: how to be loyal to our own beliefs and traditions while also respecting and accepting those different from ours. On a day-to-day level, laugh more at the inevitable foibles we all have and the mistakes we all make—especially at your own mistakes. Since imperfection is the rule, tolerance is all the more essential. Understand and accept your parents more fully—they and all parents everywhere are doing the best they can with what they know. Criticize your children less and teach them more. Especially teach them tolerance—and hope they will be tolerant of you as they grow and mature.

If possible, move beyond mere tolerance. View people's differences as the rich and rewarding experience of being human. Remember that the test of tolerance is when you are in the majority. Courage is tested when you are in the minority. Let charity, compassion, friendship, and empathy replace discrimination, bigotry, envy, and jealousy. Be not resentful of others for their capabilities and their possessions—no one has everything. Tolerance for both the haves and the have-nots is a requirement for survival in today's—and probably tomorrow's—world.

A caution about tolerance. Yet, even while we strive to be tolerant, recognize the paradox of tolerance: to be totally tolerant of the intolerant will put us at risk. Always remember that there must be limits. Without limits, all societies risk destruction. In some cases, too much tolerance risks our being trampled by the more primitive and uncivilized and unprincipled among our fellow human beings. So set limits wisely—we must endure what we are willing to tolerate. Sometimes, in trying to be humane to the primitives, criminals, and psychopaths on the planet, we risk giving license to their inhumanity.

- *Meekness. Meekness* is not timidity, cowardice, or inferiority, but rather the ability to keep feelings and emotions evenly balanced. It is the opposite of sudden anger, the holding of grudges, of rudeness and impatience. So act to mute strong feelings of hatred, revenge, and even denial so as to avoid pursuing punitive measures outside the realm of justice. This ability is the mark of all civilized societies and a vital distinction from the barbarism and savagery of more primitive stages of societal development. On an individual level and to the extent possible without capitulation, be mild of disposition and gentle of spirit. Speak up when wrongs are being done, but in a way that promotes peace. Strive to resolve conflicts peacefully, without resorting to anger and violence.

- *Patience* and *Mercy*. Fight against anger through the display of forbearance, *patience* in the face of wrath, and endurance via your ability to moderate your feelings. Show *mercy* when you can. These qualities are the antidote to anger and wrath. When possible, choose forgiveness instead of vengeance.

- *Chastity*. Curb or at least moderate the excessive indulgence of sexual desire. *Chastity* serves as a balance against and antidote to lust—and lust detracts from true love. To the extent possible without compromising your values, embrace moral wholesomeness. Work to achieve more purity of thought through education and seeking betterment of self.

Transcendence

Reach outside yourself to connect to something larger and more permanent.

- *Appreciation of beauty and excellence*. Whether being thrilled by music, art, drama, film, science or mathematics, or seeing a virtuoso performance in a sport, or simply stopping to notice the pristine beauty of a single rose, beauty and excellence are inspiring. Allow yourself to feel awed and elevated—these emotions will increase your happiness. Visit an art gallery or museum that is new to you. Pause at least once a day to notice an instance of natural beauty. Appreciating beauty evokes the same feelings as virtuous and selfless acts of kindness.

- *Playfulness* and *Humor*. Be playful and have fun and enjoy the effect on others—even by making fun of yourself. *Play-*

fulness is contagious. Life is already serious enough—some fun is a necessary balance. Lighten up in your actions and use *humor* to enliven your emotions. Make at least one person smile every day.

- *Hope for a better future.* No matter what the situation, all failures and disappointments are also opportunities. Maintain hope for a better future for yourself, your loved ones, and our planet.

BECOME BETTER BY BEING GOOD

Expend conscious and intentional effort to incorporate these traits of being a good person of good character into your life on a more frequent basis day in and day out. Focus on those traits that pack the greatest potential for increasing your life satisfaction, no matter which ones are already a part of your being. These traits are by and large ubiquitous in virtually all cultures and religions. With deliberate practice and time, exhibiting more of these traits will become a part of who you are. And, as you *become* this good person of good character, you can receive lifelong feelings of happiness just by being yourself.

SKILLS AND ABILITIES

If you plan on being anything less than you are capable of being, you will probably be unhappy all the days of your life.

—Abraham Maslow, American psychologist (1903–1982)

We all enjoy doing whatever we do well. So one final proven route to becoming a better person lies in how you choose to use your inherent, unique, and special skills and abilities over the span of your life.

Capitalize on your own skills and abilities by finding more opportunities in your life to make use of them. Identify your special abilities—everyone has some. Take stock of what you do well. Then choose an endeavor that *fits* your abilities. Find a mentor to support you. Be willing to put in the time and effort to reach your full potential based on employing and enlarging your natural abilities. Believe in the significance of what you choose to do. Don't squander your special skills, abilities, and talents—wasted talent is a sure route to disappointment and depression. Instead, maximize your abilities so you can excel and accomplish something significant in your life. Increased and long-lasting life satisfaction and fulfillment can be your reward.

TILL DEATH DO US PART

Aspire to be that person who displays virtues of both thought and action—a good person of good character who uses the full range of their unique and special skills and abilities to lead a virtuous and fulfilling life. There are no limits to goodness of character, goodness of person, or excellence of ability. In fact, many of these character and personal traits reflect the natural human desire to transcend our more primitive, biological human condition. Implementing The Fourth Imperative: Become a Better Person allows each of us to benefit from our efforts at being a better person for the rest of our lives—one of the most durable of all the imperatives. Changing who you are and becoming a better person is, by definition, permanent.

Choose to become a better person—to live a good and moral life using your natural skills and abilities as a part of your personal philosophy of life. Do this not necessarily as a part of some organized religion, although that choice is yours, not just because of some promised but unproven afterlife, and not just because doing so will make you happier—even though it will—but because to live otherwise is a violation of self, and it dooms you to remain at the lowest level of human evolution above the apes.

TRANSITION

The Fourth Imperative: Become a Better Person—a good person of good character making the best use of whatever unique skills and abilities they have—is one of the three longest-lasting of the six imperatives to implement to live a happier life. The Fifth Imperative: Embrace Loving Connections and The Sixth Imperative: Make a Meaningful Contribution are the other two.

Becoming a better person is a permanent change—and it can make you feel happier about yourself for the remainder of your life. This is not to say that your work to be a better person and to change your character and use your natural abilities to excel will be easy. But the positive feedback you will feel from yourself and receive from the recipients of your actions and accomplishments will begin a series of positive moments that will allow you to feel happier each day. And these feelings will provide additional motivation to continue to work at becoming that better person—the goal of the fourth imperative.

The Fifth Imperative: Embrace Loving Connections and The Sixth Imperative: Make a Meaningful Contribution mark the culmination of all the happiness-increasing imperatives—and they are the two with the most potential to provide a sustainably happier life. Sigmund Freud had it right all those years ago when he said, "Happiness is love and work." Even after all this time, the truest, longest-lasting paths to a happier life are those that could have been predicted all along: actively enhancing and sustaining close, loving connections with others—spouses, significant others, family, and friends—and seeking out your calling to make a meaningful contribution to the world.

Although these last two imperatives arguably require the ▶

most effort of any of the six, they are also the most durable, the most resistant to adaptation, and the ones that offer the best opportunities for lasting happiness. Not coincidentally, they are also both very other-focused—completing the core transition in the six happiness imperatives that began with a purely self-focused pursuit of pleasure in the first imperative and has been steadily becoming more other-focused in the succeeding imperatives. Synergistically speaking, by successfully implementing the first four imperatives, you will not only feel happier, but because you feel happier, you will have a better chance of successfully implementing the final two (and longest-lasting) imperatives—achieving loving and lasting connections with others and making your unique, meaningful contribution to the planet.

THE FIFTH IMPERATIVE: EMBRACE LOVING CONNECTIONS

A life without people who belong to us, people who will be there for us, people who need us and whom we need in return may be very rich in other things, but in human terms, it is no life at all.

—Harold S. Kushner, author and prominent American Rabbi

Actively work to create and sustain loving and lasting ties to significant others—spouse, family, and friends—to enrich every phase of your life. The Fifth Imperative: Embrace Loving Connections presents the penultimate proven path—connections with others—which, when emphasized, can fill your life with lifelong love and support and joy.

Seek to establish and nurture loving, intimate connections with others. Each connection can be one of the most important and longest-lasting pathways to a happier and fulfilling life. This commonsense assumption has been demonstrated to be true: the happier we are, the more likely we are to have robust and satisfying connections with other people who care about us and about whom we care enough to share our thoughts, feelings, and life events.

Connections with others—strong social relationships of various kinds—matter for many reasons. First, they provide needed support in trying times—advice, listening, reassurance, and often tangible assistance as well—all of which increase your feelings of happiness. Second, loving connections with others are mutually reinforcing—they make you happier, and then your heightened happiness improves your existing connections and also attracts other new connections—an ever-upward spiral of ever-increasing happiness. Third, your connections fulfill the deeply rooted evolutionary need to belong and to perpetuate the species. And, fourth, the happiness you realize from your connections with others doesn't seem to diminish over time—it is immune from the force of adaptation, so that the happiness generated by connections lasts far longer than that from other imperatives.

Three major paths have been found to help people achieve strong connections and, by extension, happier lives: love, marriage, and close relationships.

LOVE

If you live to be a hundred, I hope I live to be a hundred minus one day, so I never have to live without you.

—A. A. Milne (in the voice of Winnie the Pooh),
English playwright, novelist, and writer
of children's books (1882–1956)

Love others—and allow yourself to be loved. In the end, this may be all that really matters. It is rare and perhaps impossible to be happy without love or to have love and not be happy. Love is unequalled as the most powerful happiness-producing emotion in existence. Over the course of your life, if you are fortunate, you experience an almost unlimited variety of types of love: reciprocal parent-child love, sibling love, and your own first puppy love; the passionate infatuation type of love, the frustration of unrequited love, and the mature, intimate, romantic love for a spouse; your love for your children, grand-children, family, and close friends. . . . That's to name but a few of the almost infinite variety of possible loves.

No matter what form your relationships take, love is the foundation of all of them—the emotion that makes another person feel irreplaceable and that demonstrates that you can transcend your selfish tendencies and commit to put others before yourself in thought and deed. For everyone, love is the one element that is vital for living a happy and fulfilling life. Without it, you are at higher risk of feeling worthless, hopeless, anxious, and like an impostor swimming in a sea of real people.

If a parent, love your children unconditionally early in their lives—this love is irreplaceable and gives them the psychologi-cal foundation of safety and security that shapes all future relationships. It is well known that a lack of love in child-hood can have devastating effects on the rest of someone's life. Children deprived of love value love less as adults and tend to substitute money or possessions. And, in a sad twist of fate, people who value money and goods highly tend to avoid inti-mate situations, the exact opportunities that could give them the love they desperately miss.

If an adult, choose to work to become a better person—not just because to do so makes you happier—which it does (see The Fourth Imperative: Become a Better Person)—but also because to acquire and demonstrate the traits of a good person of good character makes you more capable of loving and of being loved. Some people, of course, are naturally good—and, for them, loving and being loved is a natural happening. Others must work at it—and becoming a better person is a proven route to follow to enhance your chances for love. One caution: don't mistake sexual attraction for love—while necessary, it is not sufficient for romantic love. Too soon, the novelty wears off, the excitement and mystery wane as you adapt, and you either move on to the next pleasure or choose to risk reaching for the intimacy that's at the core of long-lasting, truly loving relationships.

In the end, nothing makes up for a lack of love. As George Sand, the French novelist, said: "There is only one happiness in this life, to love and be loved." Even with its almost indescribable potential for emotional devastation, people are still willing to risk everything for a chance—or another chance—at mature, lasting love. No matter how complete life may be in the various domains of success, health, work, money, or sex, love is the one factor that, if missing, most people would trade any of the other things for in a heartbeat. And, even though nothing is as tough a guess as love, when you get it right, love can be triumphant in its power to fill you with joy and lasting happiness.

MARRIAGE

> *In fact, there are few stronger predictors of happiness than a close, nurturing, equitable, intimate, lifelong companionship with one's best friend.*
>
> —David G. Myers, author of *The Pursuit of Happiness*

Seek and hold sacred an intimate, enduring, equitable, affectionate marriage—it is an important source of strength and comfort in today's uncertain world—and the married are happier than anyone else in all countries and every ethnic group. Similarly, cultivate and cherish close, loving, nurturing, and intimate relationships with significant others—they are a balm to the soul in turbulent times. Marriage—or romantic love with a significant other—is a more potent happiness-producing activity than satisfaction with other close relationships or with work or wealth.

So find and marry the right partner—and marry for love. Marriage is a strong buffer against depression, loneliness, misery, and the everyday hazards of life. It can offer multiple roles to bolster self-worth—allowing you to feel that you are not only a valuable worker but also a good spouse and a good parent. Make sure you treat your spouse at least as well as you treat your best friend—the happiest marriages are also strong friendships.

Even if you are in a solid, committed romantic relationship, work constantly at improving it—it's worth it for you and for any children you may have. Marriage manuals and workshops abound and contain a plethora of proven techniques and actions that are the hallmarks of close, intimate, and happy marriages. Study, attend, learn the insights you need—and apply them to your relationship. The happiest marriages require commitment, mutual respect, and working together to keep love alive by sharing dreams and time as well as the inevitable ups and downs of life. And a good marriage is worth the intentional thought and effort needed to make it work. It not only offers you the best chance of having a happy and fulfilled life, it is valuable for your personal health and the welfare of your children. Children of couples in stable marriages who stay married do better by every known criterion than children in all other arrangements.

Establish and hold realistic expectations for your spouse and your marriage. Unfortunately, even a happy, loving marriage by itself is not a panacea. No matter how good your marriage is or how hard you work at it, no one magic factor can guarantee a happy life. And those with the highest expectations for marital bliss risk the biggest fall in happiness. To expect perfection from your spouse and a state of constant, uninterrupted joy in your marriage is to invite disappointment and disillusionment. Even the love of the most supportive spouse can't stave off occasional feelings of doubt, fear, and insecurity or grant you immunity from loneliness or depression. Neither can it free you from the basic human development tasks everyone must do: growing as a person, deciding what you believe in and what kind of person you will be, and acting on your beliefs to achieve your goals. All are challenges that everyone must conquer alone. In addition, the happiness a good marriage can bestow is apt to be out of reach for those who marry for money instead of love, who use pregnancy to force marriage, who have children too soon, or who adopt an unfulfilling domestic role in the marriage.

But don't let its limitations deter you in your quest for a loving marriage. Nothing is perfect. If you are not married, don't shrink from commitment forever. It's worth repeating: the married are happier and healthier than the single in nearly every country. Seek potential mates who share similar interests, activities, music, ideas, and desires—kindred spirits are more likely to become soul mates. And if your first marriage ends through divorce or death of a spouse, strive to remarry eventually. Second marriages have as much potential for happiness as first ones, so keep trying. Life is calmer in a good marriage—and longer. You can have conversations with a best friend combined with the intimacy and security of a dependable companion and loving spouse for the rest of your life.

Stay in love with your spouse—to love and be loved by

your best friend gives you the best chance of living a happy and fulfilled life. Of course, if a loving, lasting, and mutually happy marriage were easy, everyone would have one. But even though it takes some work to be a happy couple in a happy marriage, there is no more direct route to a happier life.

CLOSE RELATIONSHIPS

Friendship is a sovereign antidote against all calamities.
—Seneca, Roman statesman (4 B.C.–65 A.D.)

Invest in close connections in the form of intimate, non-romantic social relationships with family and friends—they are more important to overall happiness than success at work, a high income, or any prestige you may earn. Humans have been destined from our species' hunter-gatherer days to be what Aristotle called us: "the social animals." And so we are.

Family. Look actively to forge and nurture loving, lasting, close, long-term relationships with family—brothers, sisters, nieces, nephews, and even pets—all are important to your well-being and can help you weather the inevitable difficult times. Holding family close is even more difficult in Western society with its individualistic culture of independence—but more important than ever to ward off the feelings of meaninglessness and depression that stem from lack of attachment to any group beyond yourself. Also remember that—even though the interest, help, and support you can receive from a supportive family is a major source of happiness, good families—like good marriages—are not a panacea. Although popular belief holds that having children is desirable because they make their parents happier, it turns out that, as wonderful as having children *can* be for some, overall, parenthood makes virtually no difference in total life satisfaction. Family relationships can be the source of both the greatest joy and the greatest emotional strain—and often on the same day. Nonetheless, it is worthwhile to persevere.

Friends. Prioritize nurturing, close relationships with friends. Intimate friends with whom you have empathic, trusting, supportive relationships can offer hope if you are down and help you gain new perspective. Surround yourself with friends who care as much about your feelings and well-being as they do about their own—and as you do about theirs. There are few better antidotes to unhappiness than having an intimate friendship with someone who cares deeply about you. The bonds of great friendships help you smooth over the inevitable bumps in your life road—stress, illness, loss of a job, end of a relationship, bereavement—and reinforce you when your hopes and dreams are threatened. Women in particular value a network of close friends highly. Women not only make the best friends but also turn to their friends more readily than men (no big surprise here). They more often share their intimate feelings and tend to have face-to-face friendships, whereas most men tend to limit self-disclosure and have side-by-side friendships where they participate in activities together, but often without sharing their deepest thoughts and concerns.

Do not hesitate to make the effort necessary to establish close relationships with good friends. These relationships are usually not as elusive to form or as complicated to maintain as romantic love relationships, since they don't require the perfect chemistry. Even casual conversations and trivial exchanges of information with neighbors or coworkers can have a calming effect on your moods—short-lasting as it may be. Develop feelings of empathy for your friends instead of isolating yourself—empathy can allow you to achieve great closeness and warmth. Express your caring for them and let yourself be cared for in return. Focus on what you have in common with others instead of what differences separate you—this can create a stronger sense of connection. Revel in your role as a valuable, caring, supportive friend—and seek friends with whom you can share that same type of relationship. If you find this difficult, use the same approach to friendships that is recommended for marriages: find, study, and learn how to be a better friend from the innumerable friendship manuals and advice-givers that abound.

But also be alert to the possibility that, if nurturing close relationships seems much more difficult for you than for others, loneliness can result. Although a real problem that should be addressed separately, loneliness will shut you off from close, loving relationships—one of the proven paths to happiness. If you *are* lonely, be patient with yourself—but take some positive action. Nostalgic remembrances can help—even if just writing in a diary. Volunteer for community service for a cause you believe in. Join a club focused on your interests. Discover at least one person to whom you can relate and who brings out the best in you. Just one good relationship is enough to feel connected. And, often, from one safe relationship, others follow.

YOUR CONNECTIVITY MATTERS

For everyone, loving connections—whether in the form of loving, stable marriages or close, intimate, supportive relationships with family and friends—not only fill a deep need but also are a major key to living a happy and fulfilling life.

Invest in friendships as if you are investing in your own happiness—because you are. Strive to make time to belong intimately to a few close friends who are permanent fixtures in your life—friends with whom you share your whole life instead of just selected portions. Remember, for both women and men, it is the *strength* of relationships that matters most, far more than the number. As the Aussies say, we all need mates.

In the final analysis, your connections with others are one of the most enduring of all states. Other things are far more perishable. If you are fortunate enough to have close, intimate relationships with a loving spouse and even a small circle of family and friends, to them—and thus also to yourself—you *are* somebody. Happiness is, in so many ways, other people.

TRANSITION

With the additional stability, confidence, and assurance gained from implementing the fifth imperative of embracing loving connections with others—built on top of the foundation of the first four imperatives—pleasure within limits, thinking and acting in happiness-producing ways, and becoming a better person—you will now be better prepared and even emotionally buoyed to accept the ultimate challenge of making your meaningful contribution to the world.

The Sixth Imperative: Make a Meaningful Contribution highlights the routes to realizing your destiny—to making some type of a lasting mark—even if only a faint one—that means something to someone besides yourself and is evidence that you passed this way and made the world a better place for having lived in it for a time. And if you are successful in at least pursuing your search for meaning, you will be more likely to lead a happy and fulfilled life during your all-too-brief moments on this planet.

THE SIXTH IMPERATIVE: MAKE A MEANINGFUL CONTRIBUTION

I think the purpose of life is to be useful, to be responsible, to be honest, to be compassionate. It is, after all, to matter: to count, to stand for something, to have made some difference that you lived at all.

—Leo Rosten, American writer

Seek out your calling in life—your mighty purpose. Decide what will be your unique, meaningful contribution to make the world a better place. The Sixth Imperative: Make a Meaningful Contribution presents the final powerful proven path—serving a purpose large enough to lend depth and meaning to your existence and lifelong joy to your life.

Pursue options for making your meaningful contribution for the good of the planet. Contributing to the betterment of the world—even in a modest way—heightens happiness for you by adding a sense of meaning and purpose to your life.

Your options are many. Choose to use your talents, skills, and traits working at a vocation of your choice for monetary remuneration. Embrace altruism by volunteering your time and energy and sometimes donating your money for a just cause you believe in. Pursue your avocation—an interest, hobby, or passion that you love—and then find a way to have your avocation benefit others.

Choose any or all three of these contribution options. Your choices may vary and change depending on your stage of life and on your gender. For instance, work is a major source of self-worth for both women and men. Men often define themselves by their work. Their greatest happiness comes from performing well—accomplishing their goals by making the highest and best use of their talents and abilities. Women, by contrast, more often need a balanced life for joy—success in their work and also in their personal life. When balancing multiple roles of work, marriage, and motherhood, women often use work as a stabilizing force and source of economic security. Whatever your situation and whichever contribution-making strategy you choose, using your talents to their fullest benefits the recipients of your efforts and, at least as important, makes you happier in the process.

Only you can decide how you want to contribute to the world. But no matter which option or options you choose, you need to choose wisely. Since you may spend the largest share of your waking hours in whichever meaningful pursuit you choose, your choice can significantly determine whether you'll find meaning and purpose and more happiness in your life or doom yourself to a meaningless, empty, unfulfilled existence with apathy and unhappiness as your companions.

Here are the three major options for making your meaningful contribution to the world: vocation, altruism, and avocation.

VOCATION

*The great elixir of life is to be thoroughly worn out
before being discarded on the scrap heap—a force of
nature, instead of a feverish, selfish clod of ailments and
grievances.*

—George Bernard Shaw, Nobel Prize–winning Irish dramatist
and critic (1856–1950)

Seek challenging work that you enjoy, that you can and want
to work hard at, that you are paid for, and that is meaningful
to you. The satisfaction you receive from your chosen vocation will make you more satisfied with your life as a whole—in
fact, it is more important to your long-lasting happiness than
anything else except love and marriage. Especially while you
are single, a job can be the key to a meaningful and fulfilling
life, one by which you define yourself and create a personal
legacy that gives meaning to your existence. Not only does it
add to your personal identity, a vocation lets you belong to an
organization—a community with a network of social friends
with similar goals you all embrace. You feel a sense of pride in
your institution that becomes part of your identity.

If you are currently working, create the maximum happiness and meaning from your job in the following ways:

Rethink. Rethink your perspective on the true value of your
job and the real impact it has on people. Mentally change your
view of your work so that you perceive it as a higher calling
that has a deeper meaning—a mightier purpose—work that
truly makes a difference in someone's life. If you view what
you do in a certain way, even the most mundane job or pursuit
can be seen as doing something that matters to others above
and beyond merely a paycheck. A hotel housekeeper becomes
a "Michelangelo of housekeeping." A piano tuner is seeking

to find the perfect sound. Receptionists don't just greet people and answer phones, to each visitor and caller, they are the personification of their company—creating the first and most lasting impression. Bricklayers aren't merely laying bricks, they are building homes. Nurses aren't giving meds, changing linen, and taking vital signs, they are crafting a cocoon of care around each patient. Kitchen workers can see themselves as culinary artists. Hair stylists are shaping their customers' self-images. Even the much-maligned workaholic can feel that the sacrifice of long hours at work is worthwhile and feel elevated as a result if they believe their chosen work is being done for the right reasons and makes a meaningful contribution to the world. When you feel this sense of higher or mightier purpose in your work, you've found your calling—and can find greater happiness as a result.

Re-craft. Re-craft or restructure your work, to the extent you can, to add new routines and activities that are meaningful and reduce those that are boring and uninspiring. Make sure your work uses a variety of your talents and skills, and that its level of difficulty matches your level of skill. Where possible, participate in making decisions and setting your own goals—feeling a sense of personal control over your job is one of the key traits to intentionally foster. As mentioned in the third imperative, seek opportunities to challenge yourself to achieve a flow state during your time at work—you'll be happier for your efforts. Take more initiative and volunteer for more challenging assignments in which you can contribute more and about which you can feel passionate. Passion increases motivation and fuels performance. Without an emotional involvement, over time you risk losing interest in your daily work and even in your career.

Enlightened managers in enlightened organizations can help greatly with work redesign. Done correctly, work re-crafted and restructured in these ways can increase your happiness and meaning. This can increase your performance—often as much as 10 percent to 25 percent—thus increasing your productivity and their profit: a win-win scenario.

Change. As a last resort, if your current job is not as fulfilling as you would like, and if your personal and economic situation permits, consider a change. Search for work that satisfies your need to contribute something meaningful, that engages your creativity, intelligence, and skills, and that provides connection to a community and a meaningful service to others. Optimally, your work can help define you and become an extension of who you are.

CALLING ALL WORKERS—AND THEIR COMPANIES

Contributing by working in a job where you can do what you do best will be a job you love. And a company of people contributing their best not only has low absenteeism and turnover, it also has high levels of performance, productivity, loyalty, and morale as well as a strong financial bottom line.

This imperative to seek a vocation that you view as a calling to give meaning and purpose to your life also illuminates one of life's great paradoxes: higher incomes and greater wealth have *not* resulted in significantly greater sustained happiness. As a result, make no mistake: your overall happiness with your life may depend more on choosing work you can lose yourself in and view as a calling than on any income or wealth or prestige that comes with it.

ALTRUISM

Only those who have learned the power of sincere and selfless contribution experience life's deepest joy.

—Mother Teresa, Nobel Peace Prize winner
(1910–1997)

Volunteer to support a cause or need that you have a deep belief in—one that you can view as your calling and that is a place where you feel that you can make a difference. If, instead of or in addition to your vocation, you choose altruism as your path to making a meaningful contribution, you get to share yourself with a cause and a larger community. Find at least one volunteer activity in which to get involved—when you help others, *you* feel good. Volunteer at a soup kitchen, go grocery shopping for someone who can't, support your favorite charity. Commit to caring for someone other than yourself.

The options and valid needs and vital causes are limitless. Doing something good for others makes you feel better about yourself—it enhances your self-esteem and relieves both physical and mental stress. Beyond the giving of yourself and your time, if you have the means, another proven altruistic path is to use your money to support a cause you believe in deeply. Ironically—since money in and of itself doesn't raise your level of happiness in an enduring way because you adapt so quickly to having it—spending your money on other people or on charities can have more impact on your own level of happiness than spending it on yourself. Any form of altruism—even if it's just using your wealth for the good of others—is a proven way to make a major contribution to the planet. Sharing yourself with others—giving your time, information, sympathy, praise, acknowledgment, money—gives you the gift of happiness in return.

AVOCATION

He who wishes to secure the good of others has already secured his own.

—Confucius, Chinese philosopher and teacher
(557?–479 B.C.)

Transform your avocation of choice—your hobbies and the interests that you are passionate about—into a calling with a higher purpose by adding some *service to others* component to them. By making this distinction, you can gain a greater sense of meaning and contribution from using your best skills and talents just as you are used to doing—but using them to benefit others. For example, in addition to just knitting or quilting or playing music or singing or woodworking or creating art or enjoying whatever your passions are for your own pleasure, offer the result of your efforts to other people or groups— perhaps to those less fortunate. By sharing the fruits of your chosen avocation, you can ennoble what you love to do by benefiting others in addition to yourself. Sharing with others lets you feel more connected to them and you feel greater personal happiness as a result.

MEANING AND PURPOSE

This is the true joy in life, the being used for a purpose recognized by yourself as a mighty one.

—George Bernard Shaw, Nobel Prize–winning Irish
dramatist and critic (1856–1950)

In the end, all humans ache for their lives to have meaning—to have some impact on the world, some overarching sense of higher purpose that we are living for beyond just ourselves—in order to reach our full potential for happiness. When you find this self-generated sense of mighty purpose, you feel as if you have found your calling. If your work defines who you are, do not be afraid of using yourself up in pursuit of your dreams. Using your full capabilities in service of your calling—a meaningful purpose with personal significance—can sustain you through the trials of life.

Short of blatant irresponsibility, you can even choose to completely reinvent your life and make a meaningful contribution doing something you love. This choice allows you to say, even if only to yourself: "I have made a difference and the world is a little bit better for my having lived."

Choosing any of these three routes—vocation, altruism, or avocation—to make your meaningful contribution to the betterment of the planet lets you feel ennobled and uplifted by the significance of your purpose and happier from your sense of contribution. And if enough of us make that choice, maybe, just maybe, our individual and collective contributions can counteract the seemingly endless violations of our shared humanity and the unrelenting human disputes that are a scourge on our planet.

PHASE I
PREPARATION

PHASE II
PROVEN PATHS

PHASE III
PLAN AND ACT

PLAN AND ACT

I have been impressed with the urgency of doing. Knowing is not enough; we must apply. Being willing is not enough; we must do.

—Leonardo da Vinci, Italian painter, sculptor, architect, scientist, musician, and natural philosopher (1452–1519)

The first two phases of your journey, Preparation and Proven Paths—including the presentation of the six happiness imperatives——are both complete. You are now in possession of every strategy and action known to help people live the happiest lives possible and are also armed with the keys to the kingdom to ensure success in your pursuit of a happier life.

Your final challenge, as it always is in any worthwhile endeavor, is to transform the knowledge contained in the six imperatives from concept into reality. To turn this knowledge into life-changing actions leading to a happier life, you need to commit to living a happier life as a goal, internalize (by rereading and studying as often as necessary) the six happiness imperatives, create your own personal happiness plan with your unique "house brand" of planned actions, and prioritize and manage your limited time effectively. Your goal is to focus your efforts on implementing the happiness-producing actions from the six imperatives into your daily life each and every day from this day forward.

In other words, you need to complete the four chapters upcoming in Phase Three: Plan and Act.

CHAPTER 12

JUST A REMINDER

Happiness depends upon ourselves.
—Aristotle, Greek philosopher, pupil of Plato (384–322 B.C.)

Take charge of your future now—your happiness depends on you. The promise of this book is to provide you with everything proven to help you live a happier and more fulfilling life. The underlying premise remains simple: if given the proven paths—the six imperatives for a happier life—everyone can increase their level of happiness, starting today, by using their personal happiness plan to implement the imperatives.

Once your reading is complete, your first step on your journey to a happier life is complete. After that, it's your turn to transform promise into reality. Remember: even making just the smallest move to implement any of the six imperatives into your life can make you feel at least a little bit happier—perhaps quite a bit happier, even exhilarated. So use the tools here in Phase Three to help you begin now.

DON'T FORGET YOUR KEYS

Choose happiness. Living a happier life is a worthy goal that can benefit you, those close to you, those nearby, and society as a whole. Rely on your strength of will and take personal responsibility for your happiness—but also expect to work at feeling happier: it takes some effort. Lasting happiness is like so many worthwhile goals: no gain without some pain. If you're thinking "But I don't want to work at it, I just want to *be* happy," remember that happiness is not a feeling to be awaited—passively hoping the bluebird of happiness will alight in your life. That view of happiness is simply wrong. Instead, long-lasting happiness is a challenge to take up, a battle to be waged, a goal to be actively sought by conscious and intentional planning and effort. Like any other worthwhile undertaking, a happier life is not a trivial goal and must be attained by diligent and sincere effort.

If you still resist the idea of *working* to become happier, recall that idleness is not bliss either. Even though people often yearn for days of leisure with nothing to do—and some leisure is necessary for a balanced life, of course—the seeming blessing of prolonged inactivity can become a curse as you watch the empty hours of your life trail down like grains of sand through an hourglass.

No matter what genetic "set range" of happiness you have inherited, commit to being happier. Remember that almost half of your happiness—*40 percent*—is up to you to determine. As with most challenges in life, becoming lastingly happier will be easier for some than for others. But in the same way that study and hard work can make up for a lack of intelligence, so too can intentionally working at living a happier life make up for some amount of genetic and developmental deficiencies in happiness potential.

Define what makes you happy. Balance your self-view by intentionally comparing both upward and downward. Fight against obsessive upward comparisons—they can trap you on the hedonic treadmill as you struggle in a race with the Joneses that you can never win. Respect the power of adaptation. Be comforted by the knowledge that, given time, humans will adapt to almost anything—to the bad as well as the good. Money, fame, power, beauty, talent, intelligence, and material things are not inherently bad. Some are necessary and many are desirable and enjoyable—they just don't guarantee happiness. Often, in fact, they have the opposite effect. Beware of becoming trapped in the satisfaction of self—it's ultimately self-defeating. Move beyond a focus on self to a focus on the welfare of others.

Heed the six happiness imperatives and the keys to implementing them—these give you the greatest chances for success in creating a happier life. Remember that the six imperatives represent a remarkable consensus of thought and wisdom from psychologists and scientists and philosophers accumulated over past centuries and revalidated in the past two decades. Be confident in your ability to control what you think about and how you act on a day-by-day and minute-by-minute basis. Then think and act happier each day—in fact, fill your life with deliberate and intentional thoughts and actions of the types proven to make people feel happier. Still take your pleasures, of course, but within limits. Engage more in active pursuits than in passive leisure and TV watching, which breed mindless apathy. Strive to become a good person of good character. Love others—and allow yourself to be loved. Belong intimately to people with whom you share your life—connections to others are what complete each of us. Seek your calling—whether it involves vocation, altruism, or avocation.

Search for work that, for you, would be worth doing even if no one paid you to do it. No matter how you choose to make your contribution to better the world, add a component of being in the service of others to your work or your interests or hobbies. If you are able, choose to invest your money in a meaningful cause instead of spending it on yourself—you'll be happier for it. Making a difference in your own life and in the lives of those around you reassures you that your life has not been in vain—that you matter—and that the world is a little better for your having passed through it. Take responsibility for your future and control of your happiness—you're the only one who can.

Synergy

The six imperatives clearly do not exist in isolation from each other. There are obvious synergies to be accepted and embraced as you implement them into your life. For starters, acceptance of your genetic and life circumstances limitations frees you from tilting at windmills when it comes to setting expectations for your happiness journey. Limiting your pleasures gives you more time to pursue the more lasting paths to happiness. Intentionally thinking and acting happier yields real immediate happiness and enhanced opportunities for connections and contribution. Becoming a better person—a good person of good character—attracts happy people and potentially closer relationships as well as improved work opportunities. Work or volunteering can seem more meaningful when you are in a loving relationship with a valued partner. And when you are happier at work, your relationships both at work and at home seem to go better and be more enjoyable. Implement the six imperatives and enjoy the synergistic benefits—they are a quiet balm for your soul.

STILL GOING NOWHERE

Accept what still might seem unbelievable at first: many popular and widely accepted views about what will bring lasting happiness—money, material possessions, success and fame, talent, beauty, and intelligence—are, in fact, myths of the highest order. Just look at the lessons the lives of the rich and famous really teach to the world. Consciously and continuously remind yourself to reject these myths and see them instead as false roads—as roads to nowhere. Know that no matter how much of these attributes you amass or acquire, you will inevitably adapt. They will become your new normal—and will cease to make you feel as happy as they did initially. The same is true for all of the pleasures you enjoy. By all means, enjoy them if you are fortunate enough to be able to—but do so within limits. Remember—your feelings of joy from such experiences end pretty much when the pleasurable experiences end—not a recipe for lasting happiness. In addition, you will inevitably adapt to them, meaning that the pleasures need to become more and more intense to bring the same desired results. Worse, pursuing these pleasures without any limits wastes valuable time that could be better spent implementing the other five imperatives.

Finally, realize that there is no one "secret" to happiness—no one single factor or route to guarantee a happier life. But don't let this realization cause you despair. As much as you may initially regret that your happiness journey is more complicated than just finding one simple answer, rejoice that, in reality, instead of just one, you have many options to add some amount of joy and happiness to your life every day. And they are encapsulated in the road map to a happier life that is the six proven imperatives.

WHAT'S AT STAKE

Take your pursuit of a happier and more fulfilling life seriously—it is a worthy goal especially in times of uncertainty and strife. Your success in striving to thrive is a precious gift that benefits not only yourself but also all those around you as well as the world at large—benefits that can't be overestimated.

Trust and believe that you are worthy enough to prioritize and focus your time and energy on living a happier life. First and foremost, you owe it to yourself to try to be as happy as you can. You also owe it to those around you: your spouse, your parents, your children, your friends and acquaintances and coworkers and colleagues. If you question or doubt the seriousness of this pursuit or tend to trivialize the value of being happier, just ask any spouse or significant other what it's like to live with an unhappy and unfulfilled partner. Ask a parent about the pain suffered by all if a child is unhappy. Or ask a child what it's like to be raised by an unhappy, unfulfilled, angry, and bitter parent. Ask a supervisor what it's like to try to work with unhappy, frustrated, and unmotivated employees. Then ask a worker about working for an unhappy manager. Or ask an unhappy and probably friendless acquaintance about the worthiness of happiness as a goal. Think carefully about the impact of choosing to live a happier life. Realize that because happiness has been demonstrated to be contagious, your individual happiness can affect not only you and those closest to you but also those living nearby. Individual happiness matters much more—and can have a much more extensive impact—than ever realized before.

Finally, recall your childhood: groups of young children playing together, exploring, curious about everything, giggling in wide-eyed wonderment. Compare that picture to a group of typical adults commuting in cars or trains or buses or subways: dull faces gazing unseeingly straight ahead, emotionless. What have they lost? When did they lose it? And can they get it back?

Remember that one day, you will be sitting on that proverbial rocking chair on some front porch or veranda, maybe overlooking the ocean, and a stranger will sit down beside you and politely ask: "So, what did you do in your life?"

What will you say?

The stakes are high. The price of unhappiness is steep. And life is short.

CHAPTER 13

PERSONAL HAPPINESS PLAN

We are what we repeatedly do. Excellence, then, is not an act, but a habit.

—Aristotle, Greek philosopher, pupil of Plato (384–322 B.C.)

B e expansive in your hopes and dreams for a happier life—but be detailed in your plans. Well-considered and precise plans serve as a vital compass to keep you on course amid the swirling seas of life that buffet all of us at times. Yet, no matter how well you plan, you can expect that life will intrude on even your most carefully plotted paths. Do not be dismayed. Unplanned life intrusions are as inevitable as changes in the weather.

Comprehensive planning is the best first step to help you secure more and longer-lasting benefits from your investment of time reading this book. Thus, the goal of this chapter is to help you create a detailed personal happiness plan. This plan, should you choose to create one, will include an informed selection of proven happiness-producing thoughts and actions from all six imperatives. Once you have a plan, you can then commit to incorporating the planned actions into your day-to-day routines—beginning today—to reap almost immediate increases in feelings of happiness. Even just taking positive action to write your plan will allow you to feel happier about your future as you become an agent of change in your own life.

CREATE YOUR PLAN

Follow this simple seven-step process to create your personal happiness plan:

1. Commit.
2. Review.
3. Decide what to add.
4. Decide what to subtract.
5. Write.
6. Implement.
7. Assess and adapt.

Step 1: Commit. Ask yourself: Is it really important to me to live a happier life? Am I willing to make feeling happier a priority? If so, commit to *working* to achieve a happier life instead of waiting passively for happiness to grace you with its presence. Put your commitment in writing. Go public with your wishes. Share your goals with a loved one or trusted friend with whom you have a close relationship. Ask them for their support. Public commitments yield accountability and can be a catalyst for action, spurring you on to greater success.

Step 2: Review. Reread all six imperatives. Re-familiarize yourself with the specific strategies and actions recommended in each imperative. Consider which ones you are already doing as part of your life today—and which might be added to your daily life to increase your feelings of happiness. Limit your consideration to those actions you can begin doing in the future—let go of any resentments or barriers from your past or present situation. The past is unlikely to change—and your current situation, if you are fortunate enough to have enough of the basics in your life, has only a small effect on your happiness potential anyway.

Step 3: Decide what to add. Ponder, assess, and then decide which actions you would like to add as part of your personal happiness plan. Highlight in some way all of the known happiness-increasing actions from your reading that you are willing to try to do more frequently—often on a daily or weekly basis—to see if they work for you. Decide which ones to add to your life.

Step 4: Decide what to subtract. Consider your life as it is today. Recall those actions from your reading that can actually detract from your happiness. Popular examples include too much focus on easy pleasures (which will never bring lasting happiness since you will adapt to them quite rapidly, no matter how wonderful they seem at first) and too much time spent in idleness, say, in front of the TV (too much idleness has been linked to mild depression). Then think about which activities you currently do in your life that take up valuable time that might better be spent performing the new, happiness-increasing activities. List them and estimate the time you spend on them every week. Decide which ones to subtract from your life.

Step 5: Write. Summarize the happiness-producing actions you plan to add to your life; actually write them down in list form. Then list those happiness-sapping actions that you will no longer do as much of—those that you will subtract from your life to free up time to be happier—and write them down also in list form.

These two lists will become your personal happiness plan.

Think of the actions you are adding to your life as your own special "house brand" of intentional, happiness-producing thoughts and actions that are unique to your life situation. Seek actions to try that *fit* your life and your beliefs—actions that, at least initially, you feel comfortable trying. As you achieve more happiness, you will be motivated to try additional ones that may yield correspondingly longer-term benefits. Add target dates to all planned actions and changes you plan to make. Plan which happiness-increasing actions to implement, first by month and then on a daily basis. Pick specific days on which to try the new behaviors, and add all the happiness-increasing actions you will implement to your calendar or some other tool you use to remind you of what you are doing each day if possible.

Important: identify one new proven action to try each week or even each day.

Step 6: Implement. Starting today, begin implementing into your life all the changes to your thinking and actions that you have identified and written in your personal happiness plan. Add the new happiness-increasing actions you will be doing and subtract those actions that you are going to stop doing or, at least, spend less time doing. Remember, choosing to live a happier life is labor-intensive and requires active effort, not just passive waiting, wishing, hoping, and praying.

Step 7: Assess and adapt. Periodically assess your progress on your journey to a happier life. Adjust your happiness-producing strategies and actions as needed. Notice your feelings more—and become skilled at identifying which activities give you the most positive feelings—even if these feelings are only short bursts of joy. Select these successful activities to emphasize tomorrow and in days to come. Over time, make sure you are including proven actions from all six happiness imperatives.

Remember that the most lasting feelings of happiness come from being a better person, having loving connections, and making your contribution to the world. Adjust your personal happiness plan as time goes by.

KEYS TO SUCCESS

As with all exhortations to make changes in your life, a serious pursuit of happiness includes proven keys to success that, if considered, accepted, and applied, increase the chances of successful change. Apply these keys as you first create and then implement your personal happiness plan to make it your trusted guide and daily companion on your journey to a happier life:

- Begin now.
- Choose your "house brand" of actions.
- Pursue small wins.
- Ritualize.
- Manage your progress.
- Be patient.

Begin now. Take immediate action right now to create your first personal happiness plan while the six imperatives for living a happier life are fresh in your mind. We all lead busy lives. Don't let the busyness of your daily routine drive out the time you need to plan new, nonroutine happiness-increasing activities.

Choose your "house brand" of actions. Insist on including your own unique "house brand" of proven actions in your plan. That is, strive to choose a blend of happiness-increasing thought processes, actions, and new activities from the six imperatives that *fit*—that match and enhance—your preferences, beliefs, lifestyle, personality, and life goals, both professional and personal. Remember that people seek variety—we all crave newness—so choose your happiness-producing actions with this in mind. Vary both the timing and frequency of your planned actions to keep them fresh, positive, and meaningful. To do otherwise risks the new actions becoming routine chores producing boredom rather than happiness. Be sure your "house brand" of planned actions reflects these considerations.

Pursue small wins. Focus on implementing one new, proven happiness-producing activity today. Just begin with one small change—any change will do. Consciously think happy. Try smiling more. Perform a simple act of kindness for a loved one or a stranger. Tell someone something about them you are grateful for. Just try one new action. Then notice your reactions and listen to your feelings. See if you feel happier in any way. If so, use this first small win to build confidence and momentum, prove that the action will work for you, and reinforce your commitment to change. If not, keep trying. A happier life can sprout from these small plantings if you persist—often one small win at a time.

Ritualize. Allow yourself two to three weeks to turn each new happiness-increasing thought and action into a permanent habit. Remember that it takes time and focused effort to integrate changes into your life. New actions will become familiar rituals over time, ultimately becoming just the way you are: your new normal way of thinking and acting in your life. Self-discipline is sometimes not sufficient for adopting new behaviors and breaking old habits. Creating rituals is one way to facilitate the changes you want. And, as a bonus, just the idea that you are creating new rituals will give you an immediate positive feeling of personal control.

Manage your progress. Keep your personal happiness plan close at hand, especially during the early days and weeks of implementing the six imperatives. Refer to it daily. Choose to implement multiple happiness-increasing strategies at once to give you multiple opportunities to feel happier. Perform different actions in different weeks instead of the same routine every week. Review and revise your ideas and planned actions as your experience increases. Continually analyze how you feel to determine the optimal mix and timing that delivers the greatest feelings of satisfaction. As you assimilate these new attitudes and behaviors into your life, study which ones cause you to feel happier. And then, do more of them. Actively manage your progress just as you would any important project.

Be patient. Expect to progress in fits and starts—two steps forward, one back—rather than in a smooth sequence. Neither Rome nor a new, happier life could be built in a day. Reaching but then staying at new plateaus of progress for a period of time is more the norm. For many of us, thinking or acting in these ways is new—we were never taught how to be happy. Be patient with yourself. Every change that ends up as permanent begins as something new, awkward, and strange-feeling. Stay the course.

THE CHALLENGE

Inevitably, during all major endeavors—no matter how worthy—moments of doubt and uncertainty appear. If left unaddressed, these can lead to a paralysis of thought and action and block you from achieving the happier life you desire. One antidote to these moments is to make sure, to the extent you can, that the happiness-increasing strategies you choose to include in your life are those that you *want* to do because you find them enjoyable, because you personally value them, because they match your core values and beliefs and because they seem like natural ways for you to think and act.

Choose happiness-increasing strategies you want to do so

that your motivation comes from inside instead of externally from guilt or a desire to please. You will try harder, and you will be less likely to be deterred in your quest and more likely to sustain the new actions over a longer period of time.

FINAL REMINDERS

Successful implementation of the six happiness imperatives requires sustained daily action and lifelong vigilance—just like weight loss, smoking cessation, physical exercise, or any attitudinal and behavioral change program. Commit to this level of priority for your happiness. A happier life is always just one change in thinking or one new daily action away. Committing to and implementing just one of the actions from any of the six imperatives can make you begin to feel happier. Be confident that all the knowledge you need for a happier life is here in this book. Truly, this is all there is: everything you need when it comes to planning a happier life. Create your personal happiness plan now.

CHAPTER 14

168

> *Time-use may be the determinant of well-being that is the most susceptible to improvement.*
>
> —Daniel Kahneman, Princeton psychologist

Prioritize your time as if your happiness depended on it—because it does. Unless or until there are major shifts in the number of hours it takes the Earth to spin once about its axis, the maximum time each of us has to pursue living a happier life is 24 hours per day for 7 days—168 hours—per week. Each and every week. No more and no less; 168 hours—that's it.

Time is a limited resource. And too many of us are already making too many demands on it amid the complexity, pace, and resulting stress of modern-day life. Furthermore, there is no magic formula to optimize time-use. And time is passing.

This book demonstrates that the potential for a happier life exists for you as it does for everyone—the opportunity to transcend the limitations of your genetic inheritance and the circumstances of your upbringing and of your life today with all of its ups and downs, myths, and false hopes. The paths it illuminates—the six imperatives—will aid you each and every day on your journey to a happier life.

How successfully you manage your limited time determines to an enormous degree how happy your life can be.

So, in an oddly synchronous way, your strategy becomes crystal clear: to live a happier life, you must prioritize your time—monthly, day by day, and ultimately hour by hour—to allocate sufficient time each day of each week to implement your own "house brand" of the six imperatives you have defined in your personal happiness plan. To recap, here is the proven process:

- Prioritize the time of your life monthly, weekly and daily.

- Add the new happiness-increasing activities to your life and safeguard their space on your calendar.

- Subtract—or at least reduce—the time you spend on others that don't yield happiness.

- Accomplish all of this without compromising either your home life or your work life.

- Protect the time you need on your calendar for your new happiness-increasing actions and defend it against all other demands.

Your 168-hour time limitation means you have no option other than this process. Your happiness depends on your time management discipline.

Far too many people limit their potential for living happier lives because they fill their limited and precious time with the wrong things. Don't while away too many hours on pleasure and pampering and fun only. Before you know it, hours turn into days and months and then years go by in pursuit of pleasure and fun and you're still no happier, and late at night—alone with yourself—you wonder why.

What to do? Take charge of your happiness by taking control of your time. You are the only one who can. Focus on the six imperatives—a serious reprioritization of how you spend your time on a daily basis may be all you need to lead a happier life. Just say no to old, familiar routines that don't increase your feelings of well-being—and use the time saved for those that do. Your precious, limited time, if properly prioritized and allocated, offers you the best opportunity for a happier life, a life full of meaning and joy. But you need to begin now.

Ready or not, life as you know it will come to an end someday—just as surely as night follows day. No more sunrises or sunsets—and no more opportunities to live more happily. It's trite but true: today is not a dress rehearsal—it's the grand opening of the rest of your life.

The choice of how to spend the time you have remaining is yours and yours alone to make.

We each have 168 hours per week—no more and no less. Choose wisely.

CHAPTER 15

THE BEGINNING

You are never out of the game when it comes to happiness.
—Jonathan Freedman, American research psychologist
and author

Stay hopeful no matter what your current or past situation in life may be—no one is ever out of the game when it comes to living a happier life. Even though this chapter is the closing chapter of the book, it is actually the beginning of the rest of your life. Yesterday is part of the past—you can't change it. Today will be over in a blink and can never be repeated. Tomorrow is all you have—and the clock is ticking. So neither wistfully look over your shoulder wishing your past was different nor wallow in the present if it's less than you hoped. There is too much happiness out ahead to waste time on what might have been.

A CHOICE

The choice is yours: get busy living a happier life—or not.

No matter what your choices have yielded for you in your life to date, you can still choose to pursue the proven paths to a happier and more fulfilled life beginning now. In spite of whatever life has dealt out to you up until now or whatever barriers you may encounter from now on, you can still become lastingly happier than you are today. This book provides the knowledge—the six proven imperatives—and a plan to follow on your journey.

You can choose to hear the ticking of your life clock not as a reminder of the time remaining for you nor of the time squandered on the wrong pursuits but as a wake-up call. You can begin to work toward a happier and more fulfilling life right now. Be confident that you are never eliminated from the pursuit of happiness—if you are serious about your pursuit.

But a happier life won't happen just because you know what to do to create it.

Choose to work on living a happier life. Spend more time and more energy on creating your happier future and less on understanding your past or present. Shun the myths and false paths to happiness. Permit happiness to enter by relying on yourself and your thoughts and actions. Choose to work to implement your "house brand" of the six imperatives—greater happiness awaits you if you do.

A COMMITMENT

Happiness, like so many other things in life, is ultimately about will and choice—and commitment. Commit to your goal of living a happier life. Will yourself to change your attitudes, behaviors, and time allocations. Take personal responsibility for being happier. Without a firm commitment, you will find that everyday travails and troubles can deflect you from your goal. To help, make your commitment public: share your goal of living a happier life and the actions and activities of your personal happiness plan with a trusted spouse, significant other, or close friend. Let them join and support you to make your planned happier life a reality—but make sure they are unwaveringly supportive. As with any partnership, choose carefully and wisely, lest they undermine your plans, hopes, and dreams with envy, jealousy, or betrayal of your trust.

A COMPANION

No matter where you are on your lifelong journey to live a happier life, make this book your happiness bible. Read and reread as necessary. Keep it with you as your timeless lifetime companion. Carry it as a reinforcement of your plans and goals and a reminder of your commitment. Let it provide you with clear, practical paths to follow and with inspiration and hope now and for the rest of your life. Embrace the six powerful imperatives wholeheartedly—these proven paths can enhance your life. Know that with the six imperatives in your possession, the goal of this book—a happier life for you—is within reach. Be confident that these six imperatives contain everything you need to think, be, and do to live a happier life. Be comforted by the fact that many of the actions recommended here are familiar and timeless in their applicability and can be practiced easily no matter how busy and full your life today may seem.

YOUR DESTINY

As long as you are alive, pursue happiness, straining every sinew to snare enough of it in the time you have allotted on the planet. For most, perishing without trying to be as happy as you can seems almost unthinkable. Yet, for far too many, the successful pursuit of happiness remains one of life's most elusive and unfathomable mysteries.

Choosing to live a happier life takes courage and effort. Ultimately, no matter what problems or predispositions you bring to your happiness journey, you still have ample opportunity to live a happier life. Your choices today determine your happiness tomorrow. You are a product of your past—but you are not its prisoner—and, more important, within some limits, you are definitely the designer of your destiny.

Be bold in your plans and persistent in your implementation of the six imperatives. Make living a happier life a priority and do not be denied in your pursuit. If life intrudes on your plans, be gentle with yourself—and keep trying. Great masterpieces are rarely painted in one sitting. Perseverance carries the day.

Don't put off taking action to secure a happier life until tomorrow. Begin your journey today.

Begin it now.

ACKNOWLEDGMENTS

First and foremost, I am forever grateful to my beloved wife, whose unflagging and loving support has helped take this book from dream to reality.

In addition, I owe an incalculable debt of gratitude to the work of the leading lights of happiness study who have come before me, many of whom are named in the Suggested Readings list in the Appendix.

I stand on their shoulders.

In particular, Sonja Lyubomirsky took her valuable time multiple times in her busiest moments to patiently answer my early questions, and I will always be appreciative.

Beyond these luminaries of the psychology world, I would like to thank the following for their time, assistance, and advice during my journey to publication: Bruce Raskin, Nicole Straight, Lewis Schiff, Hilary Powers, Nancy Steele, Dick Margulis, Peggy Zukin, Elfreide Stahl, Mary Pat Panighetti, Cornelia Staub, Mark Gelotte, Marcella Macartney, Aileen Brodsky, Joel Friedlander, Corvus Meachen, Rita Redfern, Domini Collins, Bo Caldwell, Joshua Tallent, Michele DeFilippo, Rami Wazni, Jules Robbins, AnnMarie Valle, Katie Soden, Zach Crawford, and Amy Zullo.

AUTHOR'S NOTES

The Serious Pursuit of Happiness is the culmination of a more than 10-year researching and writing odyssey. My humble hope is that this book can provide a timeless gift to help people live happier lives—to cope with the realities of life today and tomorrow and to transcend their life situation both in the past and now. My wish is for this book to act as a warm comforter against the chill of life—a timeless respite from everyday stress—and a retreat to which readers can withdraw repeatedly to recharge their batteries and then emerge refortified and once again ready for the day-to-day, up-and-down tumble that is life.

My contribution is to analyze and then synthesize the accumulated research findings and additional wisdom of the ages, distilling the essence of it down into strategies and actions to make it accessible to readers the world over. No doubt more will be revealed by the researchers and practitioners of positive psychology in the upcoming years as more and more people pursue the keys to living a more positive life beyond the simple relief of psychological distress.

At its best, this book offers a set of ideals, strategies, and tools to not only help cope with life's incessant trials and uncertainties—all summarized in one simple, caring book with inspirational advice based on scientific research on virtually every page—but also on how to create and then live a happier and more fulfilling life.

Please remember, though, that no one book, no matter how well intended, can be all things to all people. If you find at any time that your own unique, possibly more deeply seated barriers to living a happier life go beyond the scope of this book and are holding you back from the life you desire, please seek professional assistance from a positive psychologist, a traditional psychologist, a psychiatrist, or another appropriate medical professional. For the time being, a blend of positive psychology interventions combined with traditional psychological analysis and treatment may be the best path—at least until some future time when both branches of psychology are united into one holistic field of study and treatment.

For the future, I suspect that, as time goes by and positive psychologists and neuroscientists around the world continue to investigate the intricacies of our genetic inheritance and the innermost workings of our brains, we will all find out that we are, maybe more than we've ever dreamed possible, truly our parents' children and evolutionary products of our species. If borne out over time, this reality will make the proven tools in this book even more valuable as we each strive to carve out our unique "house brand" version of a happier life for ourselves—with maybe even less latitude than we have today to influence the outcome.

And so, my simple wish—as well as my life's dream for writing—is to help as many people as possible live happier and more fulfilling lives—while also helping to popularize the new and promising field and research of positive psychology.

I feel privileged that you've chosen to share your valuable time with me and to trust I can help you on your journey to a higher level of personal happiness and fulfillment. In return for devoting a relatively brief moment of your life's time to reading this book, you now possess a gift that will last you a lifetime.

Congratulations and sincere best wishes on your journey to a happier and more fulfilling life.

APPENDIX

To keep the book focused on prescriptively recommending proven actions—just telling you what to do—and to not distract you from your primary goal of building a happier life, I chose to omit what would otherwise have been a constant stream of citations and references. The chapters include enough information about the study-validated benefits for you to choose which recommendations you will implement into your day-to-day life in order to be happier and more fulfilled.

In this Appendix, I provide beginning lists of the major selected books and significant scholarly research studies that underpin my recommendations, so you can go further if you wish to explore the scientific basis for the recommended happiness strategies and actions. For even more in-depth academic knowledge, you should consider pursuing the master's program (MAPP—Master of Applied Positive Psychology) at the University of Pennsylvania if appropriate in your situation.

SUGGESTED READINGS

The books listed here contain details of the findings from the substantial body of scientific research that is the basis for the recommendations in the book. You will notice that, while some books deal with the overall umbrella topic of happiness, many others focus on one specific aspect of it. I expect that the literature will see this one-topic-only focus increase as more and more positive psychology researchers continue to add additional validation to the specific strategies and actions proven to lead to a happier and more fulfilling life.

This reading list is consistent with the recommendations in the book and should offer you an even more comprehensive view of happiness and what science has shown is necessary to achieve it.

Ben-Shahar, Tal, Ph.D. *Happier: Learn the Secrets to Daily Joy and Lasting Fulfillment.* McGraw-Hill, 2007.

Csikszentmihalyi, Mihaly. *Flow: The Psychology of Optimal Experience.* Harper and Row, 1990.

Diener, Ed, and Robert Biswas-Diener. *Happiness: Unlocking the Mysteries of Psychological Wealth.* Blackwell Publishing, 2008.

Emmons, Robert. *Thanks! How The New Science of Gratitude Can Make You Happier.* Houghton Mifflin Company, 2007.

Fredrickson, Barbara L., Ph.D. *Positivity: Top-Notch Research Reveals the 3-to-1 Ratio That Will Change Your Life.* Three Rivers Press, 2009.

Goleman, Daniel A. *Emotional Intelligence: The 10th Anniversary Edition; Why It Can Matter More Than IQ.* Bantam Books, 2005.

Hatfield, Elaine, John T. Cacioppo, and Richard L. Rapson. *Emotional Contagion: Studies in Emotion and Social Interaction.* Cambridge University Press, 1994.

Kashdan, Todd, Ph.D. *Curious? Discover the Missing Ingredient to a Fulfilling Life.* HarperCollins Publishers, 2009.

Lyubomirsky, Sonja. *The How of Happiness: A Scientific Approach to Getting the Life You Want.* The Penguin Press, 2007.

Myers, David G. *The American Paradox: Spiritual Hunger in an Age of Plenty.* Yale University Press, 2000.

Myers, David G., Ph.D. *The Pursuit of Happiness: Discovering the Pathway to Fulfillment, Well-Being, and Enduring Personal Joy.* Avon Books, 1992.

Peterson, Christopher. *A Primer in Positive Psychology.* Oxford University Press, 2006.

Seligman, Martin E. P., Ph.D. *Authentic Happiness: Using the New Positive Psychology to Realize Your Potential for Lasting Fulfillment.* The Free Press, 2002.

Seligman, Martin, E. P., Ph.D. *Learned Optimism: How to Change Your Mind and Your Life.* Pocket Books, 1990, 1998.

SIGNIFICANT STUDIES

The major significant studies described in this section will give you an additional beginning to enhance your knowledge of more of the key research upon which my findings and recommended actions are based.

Ekman, Paul, Richard J. Davidson, and Wallace V. Friesen. "The Duchenne Smile: Emotional Expression and Brain Physiology II." *Journal of Personality and Social Psychology* 58, no. 2 (1990): 342–353.

Emmons, R. A., and M. E. McCullough. "Counting Blessings Versus Burdens: An Experimental Investigation of Gratitude and Subjective Well-Being in Daily Life." *Journal of Personality and Social Psychology* 84, no. 2 (2003): 377–389.

Fowler, James H., and Nicholas A. Christakis. "Dynamic Spread of Happiness in a Large Social Network: Longitudinal Analysis Over 20 Years in the Framingham Heart Study." *British Medical Journal,* 2008, 337: a2338.

Lykken, David, and Auke Tellegen. "Happiness is a Stochastic Phenomenon." *Psychological Science* 7, no. 3 (1996): 186–189.

Lyubomirsky, Sonja, Laura King, and Ed Diener. "The Benefits of Frequent Positive Affect; Does Happiness Lead to Success?" *Psychological Bulletin* Vol. 131, no. 6 (2005): 803–855.

Strack, Fritz, Leonard Martin, and Sabine Stepper. "Inhibiting and Facilitating Conditions of the Human Smile: A Nonobtrusive Test of the Facial Feedback Hypothesis." *Journal of Personality and Social Psychology* Vol. 54 (1988): 768–777.

Suedfeld, P. and R. A. Borrie. "Health and therapeutic applications of chamber and flotation restricted environmental stimulation therapy (REST)." *Psychology and Health* (1999), 14:545—566.

Veenhoven, R. *World Database of Happiness: Correlates of Happiness: 7837 Findings from 603 Studies in 69 Nations 1911–1994* (Vols. 1-3) Rotterdam, The Netherlands: Erasmus University, 1994.

To continue your study beyond this list, please see the more exhaustive and comprehensive endnotes in most of the books, as well as the detailed references listed at the end of each study. As the burgeoning new field of positive psychology continues to expand, more studies are being completed almost daily.

One final reminder. While gaining additional knowledge about happiness and how to achieve it is certainly desirable, don't let *knowing* more substitute for or become a barrier to *doing* what you need to do to live a happier life. If you've read this far, you already have everything you need to know to lastingly increase your level of well-being. Begin implementing your personal happiness plan now.

INDEX

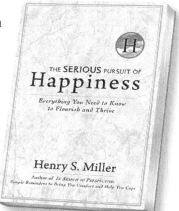

If you enjoyed,

THE SERIOUS PURSUIT OF

Happiness

please look for:

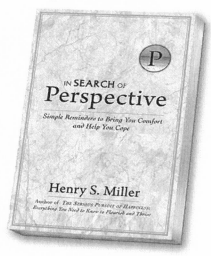

also by
Henry S. Miller

Available from:

Made in the USA
Lexington, KY
28 April 2014